HEBREWS

Chapters 8—13

J. Vernon McGee

THOMAS NELSON PUBLISHERS

Nashville

Published in Nashville, Tennessee, by Thomas Nelson, Inc., and distributed in Canada by Lawson Falle, Ltd., Cambridge, Ontario.

"Turn Your Eyes Upon Jesus" by Helen Lemmel. Copyright ©1922. Renewal 1950 by Helen Lemmel. Assigned to Singspiration, Inc. Used by permission.

Scripture quotations are from the KING JAMES VERSION of the Bible.

Library of Congress Cataloging-in-Publication Data

McGee, J. Vernon (John Vernon), 1904–1988
   [Thru the Bible with J. Vernon McGee]
   Thru the Bible commentary series / J. Vernon McGee.
      p.   cm.
   Reprint. Originally published: Thru the Bible with J. Vernon McGee. 1975.
   Includes bibliographical references.
   ISBN 0-8407-3305-4
   1. Bible—Commentaries. I. Title.
BS491.2.M37   1991
220.7′7—dc20   90–41340
                                      CIP

Printed in the United States of America

1 2 3 4 5 6 7 — 96 95 94 93 92 91

CONTENTS

HEBREWS—Chapters 8—13

PREFACE

The radio broadcasts of the Thru the Bible Radio five-year program were transcribed, edited, and published first in single-volume paperbacks to accommodate the radio audience.

There has been a minimal amount of further editing for this publication. Therefore, these messages are not the word-for-word recording of the taped messages which went out over the air. The changes were necessary to accommodate a reading audience rather than a listening audience.

These are popular messages, prepared originally for a radio audience. They should not be considered a commentary on the entire Bible in any sense of that term. These messages are devoid of any attempt to present a theological or technical commentary on the Bible. Behind these messages is a great deal of research and study in order to interpret the Bible from a popular rather than from a scholarly (and too-often boring) viewpoint.

We have definitely and deliberately attempted "to put the cookies on the bottom shelf so that the kiddies could get them."

The fact that these messages have been translated into many languages for radio broadcasting and have been received with enthusiasm reveals the need for a simple teaching of the whole Bible for the masses of the world.

I am indebted to many people and to many sources for bringing this volume into existence. I should express my especial thanks to my secretary, Gertrude Cutler, who supervised the editorial work; to Dr. Elliott R. Cole, my associate, who handled all the detailed work with the publishers; and finally, to my wife Ruth for tenaciously encouraging me from the beginning to put my notes and messages into printed form.

Solomon wrote, ". . . of making many books there is no end; and much study is a weariness of the flesh" (Eccl. 12:12). On a sea of books that flood the marketplace, we launch this series of THRU THE BIBLE with the hope that it might draw many to the one Book, *The Bible*.

J. Vernon McGee

The Epistle to the

HEBREWS

INTRODUCTION

The Epistle to the Hebrews is of such importance that I rank it beside the Epistle to the Romans (which is excelled by no other book). I have wondered how to give this magnificent Epistle to the Hebrews the introduction it deserves. Before me are excellent expository works that other men have written, and I have decided to let four of them introduce this Epistle to the Hebrews to you since each of them makes statements that are all-important. They have said what I would like to say. First I will quote from G. Campbell Morgan's book, *God's Last Word to Man:*

> The letter to the Hebrews has an especial value today because there is abroad a very widespread conception of Christ which is lower than that of the New Testament. To illustrate what I mean by this, a recent writer has said:

> "One of the best things we can say about human nature is this, that whenever a situation occurs which can only be solved by an individual 'laying down his life for his friends,' some heroic person is certain to come forth, sooner or later, and offer himself as the victim—a Curtius to leap into the gulf, a Socrates to drink the hemlock, a Christ to get himself crucified on Calvary."

> I am not proposing to discuss that at any length, but at once say that to place Christ in that connection is to me little short of

blasphemy. We may properly speak of "a Curtius," "a Socrates," but when we speak of "a Christ," our reference to Him is not only out of harmony with the New Testament presentation, but implicitly a contradiction of what it declares concerning the uniqueness of His Person.

This is a tremendous beginning for the Epistle to the Hebrews.

Dr. William Pettingill, in his book *Into the Holiest: Simple Studies in Hebrews,* has a different emphasis in his opening statement:

> From Adam to Moses, through 2500 years, and from Moses to Malachi, through 1100 years, the prophets were speaking for God to man. But at the end of the 3600 years their revelation of God was only partial. Then after a silence of 400 years, when the fulness of the time was come, God sent forth His Son, and in that Son the revelation of God is perfect.

That is another tremendous statement.

Now I'm going to give a third introduction to the Epistle to the Hebrews. It comes from the excellent book by E. Schuyler English, *Studies in The Epistle to the Hebrews:*

> The Epistle to the Hebrews, one of the most important books of the New Testament in that it contains some of the chief doctrines of the Christian faith, is, as well, a book of infinite logic and great beauty. To read it is to breathe the atmosphere of heaven itself. To study it is to partake of strong spiritual meat. To abide in its teachings is to be led from immaturity to maturity in the knowledge of Christian truth and of Christ Himself. It is to "go on unto perfection."

And here is a further statement:

> The theme of the Epistle to the Hebrews, the only book of the New Testament in which our Lord is presented in His high

priestly office, is the supreme glory of Christ, the Son of God and Son of man.

This is tremendous!

Now I turn to the fourth author, Sir Robert Anderson, and quote from his book, *The Hebrews Epistle in the Light of the Types.* As we go through this epistle I trust I shall be able to emphasize this which he emphasizes so well, and I also trust that this introduction will clarify the thought:

> That the professing Church on earth is "the true vine"—this is the daring and impious lie of the apostasy. That it is "the olive tree" is a delusion shared by the mass of Christians in the churches of the Reformation. But the teaching of Scripture is explicit, that Christ Himself is the vine, and Israel the olive. For "God hath NOT cast away His people whom He foreknew."

This Epistle to the Hebrews was not accepted by the Western church for a long time, and the reason is found at this particular juncture: the church wanted to usurp the place of Israel. They adopted all the promises God had made to Israel and spiritualized them, applying them to themselves and rejecting God's purposes in the nation Israel. As a result, you'll find that the church in those early days became actually anti-Semitic and persecuted the Jew! Therefore, to say that God is through with the nation Israel is a sad blunder, and I trust that this episode may be helpful in our understanding the great truth that a Hebrew is a Hebrew, and when he becomes a Christian, he is still a Hebrew. When any person becomes a child of God, it does not change his nationality at all, but it brings him into a new body of believers called the church. Today God is calling out of both Jews and Gentiles a people for His name. When that is consummated, God will take His church out of this world, and He will pursue His purpose with the nation Israel, fulfilling all of His promises to them and through them to the gentile world in that day. I am indebted to these four wonderful expositors of the Word of God for helping us to get on the springboard so that we can plunge into the water of the Word.

The human author of the Epistle to the Hebrews has always been a moot question. Although the Authorized Version has the heading, "Epistle of Paul the Apostle to the Hebrews," there is still a question as to authorship. The Revised Version and other later versions correct this and simply entitle it the Epistle (or letter) to the Hebrews. If you are acquainted with the literature of the Scriptures, you recognize that there is no unanimity of thought and no agreement as to who is the author of this epistle. When I was a seminary student, I wrote a thesis on the authorship of Hebrews, and I attempted to sustain the position that the apostle Paul is the author.

When I wrote my thesis I thought I had solved the problem and that the world would be in agreement that Paul wrote Hebrews! But I find that there is just as much disagreement today about the authorship as there was before I wrote my thesis! Neither John Calvin nor Martin Luther accepted Paul's authorship, and neither did many others of the past. On the other hand, many do accept Paul as the author. However, the human author is not the important thing, but the fact that the Epistle to the Hebrews is part of God's inspired Word is important.

In spite of the fact that the Pauline authorship cannot be stated in a dogmatic fashion, there is abundant evidence that Paul was the author. Both internal and external evidence support the authorship of Paul. The writer had been in bonds (see Heb. 10:34). He wrote from Italy (see Heb. 13:24). His companion was Timothy (see Heb. 13:23). The writing is Pauline. Also, in my opinion, Peter identifies Paul as the writer (see 2 Pet. 3:15–16). I believe that there is good and sufficient reason for Paul's changing his style and for not giving his name in the epistle. I'll call attention to these things as we go along. (See the Appendix for a full treatment of the subject of authorship.)

The date of writing is particularly important in the case of the Epistle to the Hebrews because of the authorship question. Many scholars, even sound scholars, have taken the position that it was written after A.D. 70. Some give the date of A.D. 85, A.D. 96, and others up in the 90s. However, as you read this epistle, you are forced to the conclusion that the temple at Jerusalem was still standing at the time it was written. This means it had to have been written before A.D. 70, since Titus the Roman destroyed the temple in A.D. 70 and Paul had already gone to be with the Lord. I believe that it was written by the apostle Paul and it was written before A.D. 70.

Coleridge said that Romans revealed the *necessity* of the Christian faith but that Hebrews revealed the *superiority* of the Christian faith. This thought, running all the way through, is expressed in the use of the comparative word *better,* which occurs thirteen times. The Epistle to the Hebrews tells us that the Law was good, but that grace, under Christ, is better and that the glory that is coming is going to be the best. The Epistle to the Hebrews presents that which is better. The word *perfect* occurs fifteen times (with cognate words). It is an epistle that challenges us. *Let us* occurs thirteen times, and *let* occurs five times.

Two verses especially convey to us this "better" way: "Wherefore, holy brethren, partakers of the heavenly calling, consider the Apostle and High Priest of our profession, Christ Jesus" (Heb. 3:1). We are to *consider* Him. Then in Hebrews 12:3 we read the challenge: "For consider him that endured such contradiction of sinners against himself, lest ye be wearied and faint in your minds." That is exactly what we are going to do as we study the Epistle to the Hebrews. We are going to *consider* Him, the Lord Jesus Christ. I am convinced that that is the most important thing which any Christian can do.

OUTLINE

I. Christ Better Than Old Testament Economy, Chapters 1—10
(Doctrinal)
  A. Christ Is Superior to Prophets, Chapter 1:1–3
  B. Christ Is Superior to Angels, Chapters 1:4—2:18
    1. Deity of Christ, Chapter 1:4–14
    2. Humanity of Christ, Chapter 2:1–18
       1st Danger Signal: Peril of Drifting, Chapters 2:1-4
  C. Christ Is Superior to Moses, Chapters 3:1—4:2
     2nd Danger Signal: Peril of Doubting, Chapters 3:7—4:2
  D. Christ Is Superior to Joshua, Chapter 4:3–13
  E. Christ Is Superior to Levitical Priesthood, Chapters 4:14—7:28
    1. Our Great High Priest, Chapter 4:14–16
    2. Definition of a Priest, Chapters 5:1–10
       3rd Danger Signal: Peril of Dull Hearing, Chapter 5:11–14
       4th Danger Signal: Peril of Departing, Chapter 6:1-20
    3. Christ Our High Priest after Order of Melchizedek, Chapter 7:1–28
      a. Christ Is Perpetual Priest, Chapter 7:1–3
      b. Christ Is Perfect Priest, Chapter 7:4–22
      c. Christ in His Person Is Perpetual and Perfect Priest, Chapter 7:23–28
  F. Christ as Our High Priest Ministers in Superior Sanctuary by Better Covenant Built upon Better Promises, Chapters 8:1—10:39
    1. True Tabernacle, Chapter 8:1–5
    2. New Covenant, Better than the Old, Chapter 8:6–13
    3. New Sanctuary, Better than the Old, Chapter 9:1–10
    4. Superior Sacrifice, Chapters 9:11—10:18
    5. Encouragement, Chapter 10:19–25
       5th Danger Signal: Peril of Despising, Chapter 10:26-39

II. **Christ Brings Better Benefits and Duties, Chapters 11—13**
(Practical)
   A. Faith, Chapter 11:1–40
   B. Hope, Chapter 12:1–29
      1. The Christian Race, Chapter 12:1–2
      2. Believers Are Now in Contest and Conflict, Chapter 12:3–14
      6th Danger Signal: Peril of Denying, Chapter 12:15–29
   C. Love, Chapter 13:1–25
      1. Secret Life of Believers, Chapter 13:1–6
      2. Social Life of Believers, Chapter 13:7–14
      3. Spiritual Life of Believers, Chapter 13:15–19
      4. Benediction, Chapter 13:20–25

CHAPTER 8

THEME: *The true tabernacle; the New Covenant is better than the old*

The high watermark of this magnificent epistle is before us in this chapter—actually it began in the previous chapter at verse 25: "Wherefore he is able also to save them to the uttermost that come unto God by him, seeing he ever liveth to make intercession for them." This verse is the key to this section. You see, the emphasis is upon the fact that the Lord Jesus Christ is living. He is not dead—He is not on a cross; He is not lying in a grave. He arose from the dead, and the emphasis is upon our living Christ. Then verse 26: "For such an high priest became us [He is what we need], who is holy [in His relation to God], harmless [He never does anything to harm—He is never moved by anger], undefiled [free from any moral impurity], separate from sinners [in His life and character, although He is right down here among us and wants us to come to Him], and made higher than the heavens [He is in the presence of God]." The value of His sacrifice is stated in verse 27: "Who needeth not daily, as those high priests, to offer up sacrifice, first for his own sins, and then for the people's: for this he did once, when he offered up himself." His sacrifice was not of silver or gold or bulls or goats; He offered up *Himself!* There is nothing of greater value than He. Verse 28: "For the law maketh men high priests which have infirmity; but the word of the oath, which was since the law, maketh the Son, who is consecrated for evermore." You do not place your confidence in a mere man when you place your confidence in Jesus; you place your confidence in the Godman. Because He is a man, He can sympathize with you and is able to meet your need. He is a royal priest. He is a righteous priest. He is a peace-promoting priest. He is a personal priest—He is *for you* personally. He didn't inherit the office; that is, He didn't come in the line of Aaron. He is an eternal priest.

Now here in chapter 8 we are told that He ministers in a superior

sanctuary by a much better covenant, which is built upon better promises.

THE TRUE TABERNACLE

**Now of the things which we have spoken this is the sum:
We have such an high priest, who is set on the right
hand of the throne of the Majesty in the heavens [Heb.
8:1].**

"This is the sum." He is not actually summing this up, although that
thought is included. He is doing more than that. Let me give you a
literal translation: "In consideration of the things which are spoken,
this is the focal (chief) point. We have such an high priest, who sat
down in the heavens on the right hand of the Majesty." As we have
said, this is the high watermark of Hebrews.

"Who is set on the right hand of the throne." Christ did something
which no priest in the Old Testament ever did. There is not a priest in
the line of Aaron who ever had a chair in the tabernacle where he sat
down. He was on the run all the time. Why? Because he had work to
do. All of these things are shadows that point to a finished sacrifice.
Now that Christ has died, all has been fulfilled, and we do not need to
wonder if we are *doing* enough to merit salvation. All we need to do is
turn to Jesus Christ and trust Him as our Savior. He sat down because
He had finished our redemption. He asks only that we accept it.

**A minister of the sanctuary, and of the true tabernacle,
which the Lord pitched, and not man [Heb. 8:2].**

Bezaleel was the master craftsman who made the beautiful articles of
furniture for the tabernacle. The mercy seat and the golden lampstand
were of gold and highly ornate. It was all man-made, although the
Holy Spirit directed him. In contrast, the Lord Jesus ministers in a
tabernacle that He Himself has made in heaven.

Now we are going to see something that I feel totally inadequate to
present.

> For every high priest is ordained to offer gifts and sacrifices: wherefore it is of necessity that this man have somewhat also to offer.
>
> For if he were on earth, he should not be a priest, seeing that there are priests that offer gifts according to the law [Heb. 8:3-4].

This verse makes it clear that at the time the Epistle to the Hebrews was written the temple in Jerusalem was still in existence and that in it priests were still going about their duties.

> Who serve unto the example and shadow of heavenly things, as Moses was admonished of God when he was about to make the tabernacle: for, See, saith he, that thou make all things according to the pattern shewed to thee in the mount [Heb. 8:5].

It is my belief that when God instructed Moses to build the tabernacle in the wilderness, God gave him a pattern of the original in heaven, the true tabernacle (v. 2), meaning genuine.

The tabernacle in its beautiful simplicity furnishes a type of Jesus Christ (which is almost lost in the complicated detail of the temple). The tabernacle was called a tent, the sides of which were upright boards, covered on both sides with gold. It measured thirty cubits long and ten cubits wide and was divided into two compartments. The first compartment was called the Holy Place. In it were three articles of furniture: the golden lampstand; the golden table of showbread; and the golden altar where incense was offered—no sacrifice other than incense. The lampstand was a type of Christ, the Light of the World. The table of showbread symbolized Him as the Bread of Life. The golden altar at which the high priest offered prayer, spoke of Christ, our Great Intercessor. Then on the great Day of Atonement the high priest passed through the separating veil to the inner compartment, the Holy of Holies, in which were two articles of furniture. (1) The ark of the covenant was a box made of wood, covered with gold inside and outside, in which were the Ten Commandments written on tables of stone, a pot of manna, and Aaron's rod that budded. The Ten Commandments speak of the fact that the Lord Jesus Christ came to fulfill the Law, and He is the only one who ever kept it in all of its detail. Then the pot of manna speaks of the fact that He is the Bread of Life even today. Aaron's rod that budded speaks of Christ's resurrection. (2) The ark of the covenant was covered with a highly ornamented top called the mercy seat. Crowning it were two cherubim of beaten gold. Once a year the high priest placed blood on the mercy seat, and that is what made it a mercy seat. That was God's dwelling place; that is, the place where God met with the children of Israel.

Around the tabernacle was a court, surrounded by a linen fence one hundred cubits long and fifty cubits wide. In that outer court were two articles of furniture. The first was the brazen altar where all sacrifices were made. The sin question was settled there, but since saints still sin, there was also a laver where the priests could wash, signifying the cleansing from sin.

Now, the Holy Place is where the priests served and where they worshipped. We worship God when we pray, feed upon His Word, and walk in the light of His presence, that is, in obedience to Him.

No one but the high priest (and he only once a year) entered into the next compartment, the Holy of Holies. But when the Lord Jesus died, the separating veil was rent in twain—torn in two—signifying that He had forever opened the way into the Holy of Holies and the presence of God. We might say that the Lord Jesus Christ took the tabernacle, which was horizontal, and made it perpendicular to the earth so that the Holy of Holies is now in heaven—because that is where He is. And we are going to find in the following chapter that the golden altar of incense, together with the ark of the covenant, are now in heaven. They are there because Christ Himself is there.

If you had been in the wilderness with Israel, you would have seen the tabernacle in the heart of the encampment, with the tents of the tribes camped all around it. You would have seen the pillar of cloud over the tabernacle by day and the pillar of fire by night. You would have seen the priests busily running to and fro carrying on their ministry of offering sacrifices and observing all of the ritual which God had commanded.

Now all of that was a shadow of a reality. The *reality* itself was in heaven. And today Jesus is there in the heavenly tabernacle functioning in behalf of you and me.

Now perhaps you are saying, "You said that when we got to this section that the writer of this epistle would start serving porterhouse steaks. Well, it seems that we are still drinking milk, because what we have been studying so far seems very simple. When are we going to get something deep?" Well, the beefsteak is ready now, and I'd like to put it right down before you.

I'll put it in the form of a personal question. My friend, is Christ *real* to you right now? If you still like to run around in a ritual and have a nice beautiful church service (there is nothing wrong with that—don't misunderstand me), but if you think that is worship, and if you think that you are serving God by just teaching a Sunday school class or singing in the choir, I have news for you. He is trying to tell us, friend, that *Jesus* is up yonder in heaven for *you* right at this very moment. What does that really mean to you? Come now, don't choke on this steak. Don't ask for a glass of milk. Don't start running around doing little things. Let the pots and pans alone, Martha; you don't need to be handling them right now. Let's sit at Jesus' feet. Let Him be a reality in our lives. When you left the house this morning, did you take Him with you? Were you conscious of His presence? He is in heaven *serving* you, friend! Christ is your intercessor. You are to go to Him to make confession of your sin. Why is it that you are worrying your pastor to death with your problems? Why do you keep going to him for counseling? Isn't Jesus real to you today? Quit being a little baby that has to be burped all the time. Grow up! Come into the presence of the living Savior. That is what the writer is talking about. Oh, may God take the veil from our eyes, and may He make Jesus Christ—in all of His power, and in all of His salvation, and in all of His love, and in all of His care for you—a true reality!

I have been asked, "Why don't you run up the American flag? Why don't you fight corruption and lawlessness?" The reason I don't preach about those things is because I teach the Word of God, and I am trying to get folk into the presence of the living Christ. When that is accomplished, all of those other things will drop into their right places. If you walk in the light of His presence, you are going to walk with Him down the street. If you go into a barroom, Christ is going to have to go in with you. I don't know whether you would want to take Him into a bar or not. When Christ is with you, there are many things you are going to have to stop and consider. You will watch your conduct when you are conscious of the presence of Jesus Christ with you all of the time. He is the living intercessor today. He is alive.

Again let me say that the Lord Jesus ministers in a better tabernacle, the genuine tabernacle in heaven. He has made the throne of God a throne of grace, and we have been bidden to come there with great confidence and assurance that He is there. The thing you and I need to pray above everything else is: "Lord, I believe. Help Thou mine unbelief." I don't know about you, but my unbelief is bigger than my belief. We need to come to Him by *faith*. "Without faith it is impossible to please him; for he that cometh to God must believe that he is, and that he is a rewarder of them that diligently seek him" (Heb. 11:6). So you and I need to have the reality of Jesus Christ in our lives. You will not see Him with your physical eye nor hear Him with your physical ear, but you will behold Him with that inner eye and hear Him with that inner ear which only faith can open.

Oh, how wonderful this is! Perhaps you think we have bogged down in this section. No, we are in His presence. We are at the high watermark. We are walking in the tall corn now. This is a wonderful section of God's Word.

THE NEW COVENANT IS BETTER THAN THE OLD

But now hath he obtained a more excellent ministry, by how much also he is the mediator of a better covenant, which was established upon better promises [Heb. 8:6].

"He obtained a more excellent ministry." The tabernacle down here was a shadow of the real tabernacle up yonder in heaven. Christ lives up there and He can keep us saved. Somebody asks me, "Do you think you can lose your salvation?" Well, I'll make a confession to you. I would lose my salvation before the sun goes down if Christ were not up there right now. He is having a problem with me—and maybe He is having a problem with you—but, thank God, He is there. My, how we need Him!

"He is the mediator of a better covenant." We have what is known as a New Covenant today; we call it a new testament. The New Testament is actually a New Covenant which God has made, and it is in contrast to the old covenant of the Old Testament. God gave to Moses the Law, then He gave to him instructions for the tabernacle with its service. It was there that sin was dealt with. No one was ever saved by keeping the Law. No one ever came to God and said, "I have kept all Your commandments, therefore receive me." No, instead they were continually bringing sacrifices because they had transgressed God's law. The Law revealed to them that they had come short of the glory of God. The sacrificial system was all shadow. Although the tabernacle God gave to them was a literal tabernacle, it was a shadow of the real tabernacle in which Christ ministers today. In other words, so far we have seen that we have a better priest; we have a better sacrifice; we have a better tabernacle. All of this converges yonder at the brazen altar because Christ is all three: He is the better priest who ministers there. He is the better sacrifice—He offered Himself. And He ministers in a better tabernacle, for He offered His own blood for your sin and my sin.

At this point I would like to refer you to my book, The Tabernacle, God's Portrait of Christ. In it I go into much more detail, and I take the position that Christ offered His literal blood in heaven. It is my opinion that He was on His way to do this when He appeared to Mary. "Jesus saith unto her, Touch me not; for I am not yet ascended to my Father: but go to my brethren, and say unto them, I ascend unto my Father, and your Father; and to my God, and your God" (John 20:17). I think He was at that moment our High Priest on His way to offer His literal blood in heaven. And I believe it will be there throughout eternity to remind us of the price that He paid for our redemption. When my book was first published, it was reviewed by a Christian magazine. The critic recommended it but warned that I took this literal view. The critic called it a crude concept. Well, I don't think that the blood of Christ is crude—either when it was shed on earth or offered in heaven. Simon Peter, who was not what one might call a cultured individual, called it precious blood. A society dowager approached a great preacher in the East years ago. Looking at him through her lorgnette (a lorgnette, you know, is a sneer on the end of a stick), she said, "I hope you will not be like our last preacher. He was rather old-fashioned and put great emphasis on the blood. The blood offends my aesthetic nature. Don't you think it is crude?" His reply to her was, "Madam, I see nothing crude about the blood of Christ except my sin and your sin." I agree with him wholeheartedly. I say to you very definitely and dogmatically that I believe His blood is even now in heaven, and throughout the endless ages it will be there to remind us of the awful price Christ paid to redeem us.

"Which was established upon better promises." Back in the Old Testament God had given the Mosaic Law, and when the people of Israel broke it, they brought the sacrifices. *Before* God gave the Mosaic Law and the instructions for approaching Him through the tabernacle ritual, they came to God by faith like Abraham did. Then when we move back of the time of Abraham, we find that Noah was on a different basis altogether. I don't feel that you can read the Bible intelligently without seeing that God dealt with men differently in different ages. If you don't want to call them dispensations, then you use your own word, but if you accept the inerrancy of Scripture and believe it is the Word of God, you are faced with the dispensational system—if you read it aright.

The writer of this epistle says that now we have a "better covenant" and that it is based upon "better promises." Although you and I as Christians have been made a part of it, God is not through with the nation Israel, and these "better promises" are going to be fulfilled for them in the future Millennium.

When you read the Old Testament prophets, you just cannot get away from the fact that God is going to return the children of Israel to their land. (As far as I can see, the present return of the Jews to Israel is not the fulfillment of prophecy.) For example, notice this prophecy in Jeremiah: "Thus saith the LORD; Behold, I will bring again the captivity of Jacob's tents, and have mercy on his dwelling places; and the city shall be builded upon her own heap, and the palace shall remain after the manner thereof" (Jer. 30:18). Then in Jeremiah 31:8 we read, "Behold, I will bring them from the north country, and gather them from the coasts of the earth, and with them the blind and the lame, the woman with child and her that travaileth with child together: a great company shall return thither." This verse mentions the north country, which is Russia. The Jews are having a hard time getting out of Russia today, but when God steps in, there will be no trouble getting out of Russia and going to Palestine. Continuing on in the Book of Jeremiah we are told, "Hear the word of the LORD, O ye nations, and declare it in the isles afar off, and say, He that scattered Israel will gather him, and keep him, as a shepherd doth his flock. For the LORD hath *redeemed* Jacob, and ransomed him from the hand of him that was stronger than he" (Jer. 31:10–11, italics mine). The Jews are not in Israel under God's redemption today—they are far from Him. But when that day comes, there will be a fulfillment of what the writer to the Hebrews is talking about when he says that there are going to be better promises on a better covenant that God will make with these people. "Behold, the days come, saith the LORD, that I will make a new covenant with the house of Israel, and with the house of Judah: Not according to the covenant that I made with their fathers in the day that I took them by the hand to bring them out of the land of Egypt; which my covenant they brake, although I was an husband unto them, saith the LORD: But this shall be the covenant that I will make with the house of Israel; After those days, saith the LORD, I will put my law in their *inward parts*, and write it in their *hearts*; and will be their God, and they shall be my people" (Jer. 31:31–33, italics mine). In effect, God says, "I gave it to them before and wrote it on a cold hard stone—and they couldn't keep it, but now I am going to write it on the fleshly tablets of the heart." He has not done this up to the present moment. As I write this, I have just returned from the land of Israel and I saw no turning to God at all. One of the tour guides whom I had the privilege of meeting was a very attractive and likeable fellow. After I had witnessed to him, I told him, "You ought to be telling me about Jesus. You are a Jew, and you are living here in this land where He lived. He died for the sins of the world. I'm a poor Gentile who has come from afar. You ought to be telling me about Him—and here I am telling you!" He just laughed. May I say to you, friend, the Jews are not back in their land according to this promise. But someday Jeremiah's prophecy is going to be ful-filled. Listen to him: "And they shall teach no more every man his neighbour, and every man his brother, saying, Know the LORD: for they shall all know me [they don't know Him today], from the least of them unto the greatest of them, saith the LORD: for I will forgive their iniq-uity, and I will remember their sin no more" (Jer. 31:34). This is what the writer to the Hebrews is talking about. The New Covenant is estab-lished upon better promises. Christ is the mediator of the better cove-nant because it contains better promises.

> **For if that first covenant had been faultless, then should no place have been sought for the second [Heb. 8:7].**

"For if that first covenant had been faultless"—the first covenant was not adequate, which created a necessity for a better covenant. Some-body says, "Then the old covenant was wrong." Now, that is not the case. Listen to the next verse:

> **For finding fault with them, he saith, Behold, the days come, saith the Lord, when I will make a new covenant with the house of Israel and with the house of Judah [Heb. 8:8].**

"For finding fault with *them*"—not with *it*. The problem never was with God's covenant. There is nothing wrong with God's law, but there is a whole lot wrong with you and me. You and I are not able to keep the Law; we are not able to measure up to its requirements.

"Behold, the days come, saith the Lord, when I will make a new covenant with the house of Israel and with the house of Judah." We have just read about that in Jeremiah's prophecy, and you can read about it in the rest of the prophets.

> **Not according to the covenant that I made with their fathers in the day when I took them by the hand to lead them out of the land of Egypt; because they continued**

> not in my covenant, and I regarded them not, saith the
> Lord [Heb. 8:9].

The people broke the first covenant. It did not enable them to perform
what it demanded.

> For this is the covenant that I will make with the house
> of Israel after those days, saith the Lord; I will put my
> laws into their mind, and write them in their hearts:
> and I will be to them a God, and they shall be to me a
> people [Heb. 8:10].

The New Covenant will be written upon their hearts—not upon tables
of stone—so that they will be able to obey it.

> And they shall not teach every man his neighbour, and
> every man his brother, saying, Know the Lord: for all
> shall know me, from the least to the greatest.

> For I will be merciful to their unrighteousness, and
> their sins and their iniquities will I remember no more
> [Heb. 8:11–12].

There will be full forgiveness of sin. There will be complete pardon.

> In that he saith, A new covenant, he hath made the first
> old. Now that which decayeth and waxeth old is ready to
> vanish away [Heb. 8:13].

So, my friend, we are not under the Mosaic system. God says that it is
an old model and He has brought in a new model. That New Covenant
He has made through the Lord Jesus Christ who is our Savior. Let me
repeat, He did it, not because there was something wrong with the old
covenant, but because there is something wrong with us. I feel sorry
for folk today who have come back to the old covenant. They try to keep
the Sabbath day and they try to keep the Mosaic Law. Oh, my friend, if

they will really study it and are honest, they *know* they are not keeping the Mosaic system. They come short. All of us need to come to God for mercy, and accept in His New Covenant the provision of a Savior.

The Law was totally incapable of producing any good thing in man. Paul could say, "For I know that in me (that is, in my flesh,) dwelleth no good thing . . ." (Rom. 7:18). And, friend, that is Scripture, and that is accurate. Man is totally depraved. That doesn't mean only the man across the street or down in the next block from you, nor does it mean only some person who is living in overt sin; it means *you* and it means *me*. The Holy Spirit is now able to do the impossible. The Holy Spirit can produce a holy life in weak and sinful flesh.

Let me illustrate this truth by using a very homely incident. Suppose a housewife puts a roast in the oven right after breakfast because she is going to serve it for the noon meal. Time goes by and the telephone rings. It is Mrs. Joe Dokes on the phone. Mrs. Dokes begins with "Have you heard?" Well, the housewife hasn't heard, but she would like to; so she pulls up a chair. Someone has defined a woman as one who draws up a chair when answering a telephone. Mrs. Dokes has a lot to tell, and about an hour goes by. Finally our good housewife says, "Oh, Mrs. Dokes, you'll have to excuse me. I smell the roast—it's burning!" She hangs up the phone, rushes to the kitchen, and opens the oven. Then she gets a fork and puts it down in the roast to lift it up, but it won't hold. She can't lift it out. She tries again, closer to the bone, but still it won't hold. So she gets a spatula. She puts the spatula under the roast and lifts it out. You see, what the fork could not do, in that it was weak through the flesh, the spatula is able to do. Now, there is nothing wrong with the fork—it was a good fork. But it couldn't hold the flesh because something was wrong with the flesh—it was overcooked. The spatula does what the fork could not do.

The Law is like the fork in that it was weak through the flesh. It just won't lift us up; it *can't* lift us up. But a new principle is introduced: the Holy Spirit. What the Law could not do, the Holy Spirit is able to do. Therefore, you and I are to be saved and are to live the Christian life on this new principle. We have a New Covenant based upon better promises; God has given to us the Holy Spirit and Christ, our intercessor, is up yonder to help us today.

This is a very wonderful passage of Scripture. If you want to get off the milk diet (although milk is good for you, and there is milk in the Word), learn to eat some meat along with it. The meat is to put the emphasis upon the living Christ, His ascension, and His intercession yonder in heaven for you and for me. My friend, when we lay hold on the living Christ, we have gone to the heights. We cannot go any higher than that in this age in which we live.

CHAPTER 9

THEME: New sanctuary better than old; the superior sacrifice

NEW SANCTUARY BETTER THAN THE OLD

Our subject is the priesthood of the Lord Jesus Christ who is a priest after the order of Melchizedek. Presented to us are two ministries which are in sharp contrast. The Levitical service, the ministry of the Aaronic priesthood, was carried out in an earthly tabernacle down here. That sanctuary on earth was merely a type of the one which is in heaven, the sanctuary in which the Lord Jesus is serving today. This sanctuary in heaven provides for better worship. A great many people consider the Law from the standpoint of the Ten Commandments, but the Epistle to the Hebrews approaches the Law from the viewpoint of its place of worship and its priesthood. That approach puts the emphasis on the settling of sins, and, as the writer will point out, the Law never really settled the sin question. "For it is not possible that the blood of bulls and of goats should take away sins" (Heb. 10:4).

> **Then verily the first covenant had also ordinances of divine service, and a worldly sanctuary [Heb. 9:1].**

The word for "service" here would be better translated as "worship."

"A worldly sanctuary" does not mean worldly as we usually think of it, but it means a sanctuary of this world; that is, it was made of materials of this world. It was made so long, so wide, and so high, and there was a ritual that the people went through in the sanctuary down here. In that sense it was of the world. The writer is going to further contrast it with the sanctuary that is in heaven.

> **For there was a tabernacle made; the first, wherein was the candlestick, and the table, and the shewbread; which is called the sanctuary [Heb. 9:2].**

"For there was a *tabernacle* made"—notice that we are not taken back to the temple. There is no reference made to Herod's temple for the sake of this illustration. Although the third temple was then in existence, when the type is given, the writer goes beyond them all to that very simple structure that God gave to Moses in the wilderness. "There was a tabernacle made," and it was made of the things of this world. It was patterned after the one in heaven, but it was much inferior in many different ways, as we shall see.

"Which is called the sanctuary"—that is, it was the Holy Place. The tabernacle proper was just a big gold box thirty cubits (about forty-five feet) long, ten cubits (about fifteen feet) wide, and ten cubits high. It was divided into two sections. The first was the Holy Place in which there were certain articles of furniture: the table of the showbread and the golden lampstand. Then, in the background was the golden altar, the altar of incense, which speaks of prayer—no sacrifices were ever made there.

> And after the second veil, the tabernacle which is called the Holiest of all;
>
> Which had the golden censer, and the ark of the covenant overlaid round about with gold, wherein was the golden pot that had manna, and Aaron's rod that budded, and the tables of the covenant;
>
> And over it the cherubims of glory shadowing the mercyseat; of which we cannot now speak particularly [Heb. 9:3–5].

In the Holy of Holies (which was separated from the Holy Place by a veil and into which only the high priest entered), there were two articles of furniture. There was the ark, which was just a box made out of gopher wood and overlaid inside and outside with gold, and on top of the ark was a highly ornamented top called the mercy seat. It was fashioned with cherubim, made of pure gold, looking down upon the top of the box. That was where the blood was placed, and that was what made it a mercy seat—for "without shedding of blood is no remission" of sins.

"Which had the golden censer," that is, the golden altar. Notice that a change has been made—we are told that the golden altar is inside the Holy of Holies rather than inside the Holy Place. Why has it been moved to the inside? The veil between the Holy Place and the Holy of Holies was made of fine twine Egyptian byssus linen with the cherubim woven into it, and it spoke of the humanity of the Lord Jesus. When He died on the cross, He gave His life, His human life, and at that time the veil was rent in twain. So the veil which was torn in two has been removed, signifying that the way to God is wide open, because Christ has made a way. He said, "No man cometh to the Father, but by me" (see John 14:6). The veil has been rent in twain, and we can come right into God's presence today. But what happened to the golden censer or the golden altar? It has been moved inside the Holy of Holies. Aaron on the great Day of Atonement came with the blood to sprinkle upon the mercy seat, taking a censer filled with coals and with incense in it, and he went inside the Holy of Holies. He was actually transferring, as it were, the altar of incense to the inside. He took the censer of burning coals from off the altar with sweet incense on it, and took it into the Holy of Holies, but he brought it back out again. And he had to do that again the next year and then again the next.

However, we have a Great High Priest who is our Great Intercessor always at the golden altar making intercession for us. His prayers are heard, by the way. Therefore, the golden altar is on the inside, but it is also on the outside, because you and I can come through Him by prayer. That is what Paul meant when he said, "Being justified by faith, we have peace with God through our Lord Jesus Christ: by whom also we have *access* . . ." (Rom. 5:1–2).

The writer mentions also the things which were in the ark. "Wherein was the golden pot that had manna"—this speaks of the present ministry of Christ. He feeds those who are His own. He feeds them with His Word. He is the Bread of Life. The Bible is God's bakery, and if you want bread, that is where you will go to get it.

"And Aaron's rod that budded." This speaks of the death and resurrection of Christ, because it was a dead rod and life came into it.

"And the tables of the covenant" speaks of the fact that the Lord Jesus Christ fulfilled all the law.

"Of which we cannot now speak particularly." The writer means he doesn't have time to dwell upon the tabernacle, because the things that he is emphasizing are the priesthood and worship. He is concerned about what real worship is and how we are to worship.

> **Now when these things were thus ordained, the priests went always into the first tabernacle, accomplishing the service of God [Heb. 9:6].**

"The priests went *always* into the first tabernacle." The priests went continually—they never finished the job. If they went today, they would be going again tomorrow, and the next day, and on and on and on. I am of the opinion that it must have become very monotonous over the years for a priest to continually go through this ritual. The very repetition of it meant that it was not sufficient, that is, that one time would not do. However, we are going to see that Christ went *once* into the Holy Place—it was necessary for Him to go just one time.

"Accomplishing the service of God" should be "accomplishing the *worship* of God." This was the ultimate goal of it all, that God's people might worship Him. This is speaking of real worship, not just a church service where an order of service is followed. When real worship takes place it is a worship that draws us into the presence of Christ where we can adore Him.

The word *worship* comes from the same Anglo-Saxon root word as *worth*. To worship is to give someone something of which they are worthy. The Lord Jesus Christ is worthy to receive our praise and our adoration. That is worship, and from that follows service. Real worship will always lead to service. In the midst of His temptation in the wilderness, the Lord Jesus answered Satan, ". . . For it is written, Thou shalt *worship* the Lord thy God, and him only shalt thou *serve*" (Matt. 4:10, italics mine). You will not have to beg and coax and goad people into doing something, if they are participating in real worship of Christ—because real worship leads to service. Many ministers spend a great deal of time urging people to do something—urging them to give, urging them to do visitation, urging them to teach, or urging them to sing. Real worship will lead to service. Such worship is possible only through Jesus Christ.

The ritual of the tabernacle never brought the people into the presence of God. The high priest alone went into the Holy of Holies.

> **But into the second went the high priest alone once every year, not without blood, which he offered for himself, and for the errors of the people [Heb. 9:7].**

He is speaking now of the great Day of Atonement. This was Yom Kippur, in one sense the high day in the life of the nation Israel. This is the day that the great high priest went into the Holy of Holies on behalf of the nation. And on the basis of his having done this, the nation was accepted for another year.

Our Great High Priest has gone into the Holy of Holies, into the very presence of God. He has gone in, and He has not come out. He is going to be there as long as we are in the world. When He does come out, He is coming out after His own—we are a part of Him; we are the "body" of Christ.

The purpose of all of this is to make real to your heart and mine the presence of the Lord Jesus. Did you start out the day with Him? This is a hurly-burly world you and I are in, and it has no time for Him. As you have rushed through this day, has He been with you? Have you worshipped Him? To worship Him we do not have to go to church and sing the doxology (although the writer of this epistle is going to urge us to do that because we need to be with God's people and participate in concerted, corporate worship; it is essential for our growth) but we can worship Him anywhere. You can worship Him at the end of a cotton row or a corn row. You can worship Him on the freeway. You can worship Him in the office. You can worship Him in the classroom. My friend, I don't care where you are, you can worship Him. You and I need to pour out our hearts in adoration and praise unto His holy name.

Now our High Priest has gone into the Holy of Holies on our behalf this very day. And you can see how superior this is to the past when the high priest went in on just one day each year—and didn't stay; in fact, he hurried out. Tradition tells us that he actually had a chain around his foot, because if he did anything wrong, he would have been struck dead and they would have had to pull him out and get a new high priest.

Oh, the wonder and the glory of it all! Our High Priest has gone into the very presence of God for you and me, and He is there today. Someone has given a little different translation of Hebrews 9:24, and I want to give it to you at this point: "For Christ entered not into a holy place made with hands, like in pattern to the true, but into heaven itself, now to appear before the face of God for us." Moses asked to see God's face but was told that no man could see God. However, you and I have a High Priest who has gone into the very presence of God.

We do not worship Him by going through a ritual. We do not worship Him by burning candles or incense, or by having a nice little altar fixed up. Some Protestant churches have really gotten involved in such things.

The last time I was in the church of a minister friend I asked him why he had a cross set up on the table used for the Lord's Supper. He said, "Oh, not only that, but did you notice the candles?" I hadn't noticed them, but he also had a candle at each end of the table. He said, "That's to help the people with their worship." My friend, if you need that kind of help, you are not worshipping Him. The woman at the well asked the Lord Jesus where the people should worship God, and the Lord replied, "The hour cometh, and now is, when the true worshippers shall worship the Father in spirit and in truth: for the Father seeketh such to worship him" (John 4:23). I have another minister friend who is very concerned with Jewish evangelism, and he has a menorah with seven candles on it in his church. He told me that it was to keep their minds centered on the fact that they have an obligation to the Jewish people. If we need that sort of thing in our churches, we are not really worshipping God.

Oh, that you and I could get into His presence and smell the sweet incense of His presence—not with our noses but with our hearts and our souls and our minds. I pray that I might be conscious of the sweetness of His presence, that I might walk in the light of His Word, and that there might be reality in my life every day. I covet that for you too.

We need to put away our bottle of milk with its little nipple, and we
need to feed on the meat of the Word. We need to get into the presence
of the living Christ who is our Great High Priest ministering yonder at
a better tabernacle than the one that was on this earth. We can worship
the living Christ today.

> **The Holy Ghost this signifying, that the way into the ho-
> liest of all was not yet made manifest, while as the first
> tabernacle was yet standing [Heb. 9:8].**

In other words, all of this was a picture and a type that the way into the
very presence of God (actually, right into the very *face* of God) had not
yet been opened.

> **Which was a figure for the time then present, in which
> were offered both gifts and sacrifices, that could not
> make him that did the service perfect, as pertaining to
> the conscience;**
>
> **Which stood only in meats and drinks, and divers
> washings, and carnal ordinances, imposed on them un-
> til the time of reformation [Heb. 9:9–10].**

"That could not make him that did the *service* perfect," could read
"that could not make the *worshipper* perfect."

The way to God in the tabernacle was actually blocked by the three
entrances and compartments. In other words, the people could come
only to that outer entrance and bring their sacrifice. If a man brought a
little lamb, he would put his hand on it in an act of identification since
it would die in his place, and then the priest would take it from there.
It would be slain and offered upon the brazen altar. The individual
who brought the lamb could go no farther than the entrance. Then, as
far as the Holy Place was concerned, only the priest could go in there.
And into the Holy of Holies neither the priest nor the people could go.
Only the high priest could enter in there. Therefore, the tabernacle was
a temporary, makeshift arrangement. The service of ritual and ordi-
nances was given for just a brief time.

Now Christ can bring us to God, but only He can bring us there. ". . . No man cometh unto the Father," He said, "but by me" (John 14:6). Such is real worship, and real worship will lead to service. Once we get into the presence of God, there will be no problem about serving.

Worship is something that the liberal today condemns. Years ago the late Dr. Harry Emerson Fosdick said that the world tried to get rid of Jesus in two ways—one was by crucifying Him and the other was by worshipping Him! My friend, it is blasphemy to say that if you worship Him you are no better than those who crucified Him! We approach a holy God today on the basis of a crucified Savior. He alone can cause us to worship.

That is the reason for Paul's writing to the Ephesians: "And be not drunk with wine, wherein is excess; but be filled with the Spirit." Now notice the first thing Paul speaks of after being filled with the Spirit: "Speaking to yourselves in psalms and hymns and spiritual songs, singing, and making melody in your heart to the Lord" (Eph. 5:18–19). That is worship. My friend, the greatest thrill in the world for a child of God is to be filled with the Spirit of God and to have the Spirit of God take the things of Christ and make them real to us. What joy that brings to our hearts! If you have been in the presence of God to worship, you will have joy in your heart and you will have a song in your heart. Some of us have difficulty getting that song to our lips—I always have!—but it is certainly down in my heart. It is wonderful to worship Him.

I want to recapitulate what we have said concerning the sanctuary here on earth which is inferior to the one in heaven. To do so, I will share from an outline put out by a good friend of mine, Dr. Warren W. Wiersbe (*Be Confident*). This is what we have seen concerning the sanctuary here on earth:

1. *It was on earth.* It was a worldly sanctuary, that is, it was made of earthly things, material things. It was erected on this earth down here.

2. *It was but a shadow of things to come.* It never was the reality. So many of us have things mixed up. We go back and study about the tabernacle, and we can really get our interest centered in that earthly

tabernacle. But, at best it was just a shadow, a picture of the real one that is in heaven.

3. *It was inaccessible to the people.* You just couldn't get in there. If you had been an Israelite in that day, you couldn't go rushing into the presence of God. You would have been stopped at that first entrance. You would have needed a sacrifice there, and you couldn't have gone any further—the priest served for you. However, today we are a priesthood of believers, and each one of us has access to God. That is one of the great privileges we have because Christ has rent the veil in twain. He has gone into the presence of God, into the *face* of God. He is right there, my friend, and He is there for us. The Israelites didn't have that privilege under the old covenant.

4. *It was temporary.* But the Lord Jesus Christ is going to keep the way open for eternity. I have a notion that Vernon McGee is going to need someone who will keep it open for him throughout eternity. The earthly tabernacle was only a temporary arrangement.

5. *It was ineffective to change the hearts of the people.* This is the thing I want to emphasize above everything else. The earthly sanctuary had nothing in the world to do with changing people's lives. But today you can come to Christ, and He can change your life. He alone can enable you to worship God in spirit and in truth and make Him a reality in your life. Many folk today just play church—like we played house by the hours when we were kids. I know a lot of Christians who are grown up and have gray hair, and they're still playing church. They go to committee meetings, they're on the board, some sing in the choir, some teach a Sunday school class—they are as busy as termites and just about as effective. They think they are serving God. My friend, you can never serve Him until you have worshipped Him.

THE SUPERIOR SACRIFICE

But Christ being come an high priest of good things to come, by a greater and more perfect tabernacle, not made with hands, that is to say, not of this building [Heb. 9:11].

"Of good things to come" really means good things *that have come to pass*. Oh, the good things that have come through Him!

"A greater and more perfect tabernacle, not made with hands." This tabernacle is nothing that man has built down here. The better tabernacle does not belong to this natural creation as to materials or builders.

Let me say this very kindly. All of this business today of trying to sweeten up the worship service with pictures and stained glass windows and candles and crosses ministers to the *flesh*. It is fleshly—it ministers to the physical side of man. It doesn't minister to his spiritual needs at all. We need to recognize that there is a real tabernacle in heaven; there is a real High Priest there, and there is *spiritual* worship. You can worship Him anywhere, and it is wonderful when people can come together in a church and really worship God. I'm sure many of you have been in a service like that, and it is a wonderful thing.

Neither by the blood of goats and calves, but by his own blood he entered in once into the holy place, having obtained eternal redemption for us [Heb. 9:12].

I believe this verse proves that Christ took His literal blood to heaven. If that is not what the writer is talking about here, I do not know what he is saying. "Neither by the blood of goats and calves"—that is literal blood. "But by his own blood," this is the literal blood which He shed on the cross. "He entered in." How? By His own blood. His was a superior sacrifice and the only one worthy of the genuine tabernacle.

"Having obtained eternal redemption *for us*." Notice that in your Bible the words *for us* are in italics, indicating that they are not in the original manuscript. They were added to smooth out the translation, which is all right, but they are not the emphasis of the verse. The emphasis is upon the contrast that Christ entered *once* into the Holy Place and obtained *eternal* redemption. The Israelite priests went in *continually*, and they got a *temporary* sort of thing. Only Christ went in once and obtained eternal redemption. This now puts the authority and the importance upon the sacrifice of Christ, and it reminds us that the *life* of Christ never saved anyone. You can follow His teachings and think you are saved, but, my friend, His teaching never saved anyone. It is the *death* of Christ, it is His redemption that saves.

For if the blood of bulls and goats, and the ashes of an heifer sprinkling the unclean, sanctifieth to the purifying of the flesh [Heb. 9:13].

"And the ashes of an heifer" is a reference to the ordinance of the red heifer in Numbers 19. The heifer was burned completely and its ashes kept in a clean place. When a man became ceremonially defiled (primarily by touching a dead body), the priest would take the ashes, mingle them with water, and sprinkle the offender. This served to ceremonially purify him so that he could be restored to fellowship. I would like to have you notice that here the heifer has a particular symbolism. A female, instead of a bull, is used. We are told in 1 Peter 3:7 that the female is the weaker vessel. Our defilement actually comes through our weakness. We are weak, and Christ came down and experienced physically, in the flesh, our weakness.

We are told also that a *red* heifer was used. The red, I think, speaks of the fact that Christ became sin for us—not in some academic way, but He actually *became* sin for us. How do we know that red is the color of sin! Isaiah said, "Come now, and let us reason together, saith the LORD: though your sins be as *scarlet*, they shall be as white as snow; though they be *red* like crimson, they shall be as wool" (Isa. 1:18, italics mine). So it must be a red heifer, speaking of the fact that He became sin for us.

The animal must also be without blemish. It certainly could not represent Christ unless it was perfect. He was holy, harmless, undefiled, and separate from sinners.

The red heifer must be an animal upon which a yoke had never been put. This symbolizes the fact that although Christ was made sin for us, He was never under the bondage of sin.

The heifer was to be led outside the camp and there slain before the high priest. In this we have pictured that the Lord Jesus is both the offering and the High Priest—He offered Himself.

The blood of the offering was to be sprinkled by the high priest before the tabernacle seven times. Many people think that seven is the number of perfection in Scripture. That is only indirectly true; the primary meaning is completeness. It speaks here of the fact that Christ's sacrifice is a *finished* transaction—one sacrifice takes care of the sin of the believer.

The carcass of the heifer was to be burned—again in the sight of the high priest. You see, God so loved the world that He *gave* His only begotten Son. Jesus freely gave Himself, but we probably have never thought of the sorrow that was in heaven the day He died.

Numbers also tells us that cedar and hyssop were to be put with the sacrifice. This is rather suggestive to me. First Kings 4:33 says, "And he [Solomon] spake of trees, from the cedar tree that is in Lebanon even unto the hyssop that springeth out of the wall. . . ." Solomon ran the gamut of trees and plant life; he was a dendrologist and knew the entire field. I think this is what Isaac Watts meant by "the whole realm of nature." Therefore I believe this speaks of the fact that the Lord Jesus Christ not only redeemed mankind, but He has redeemed this world. We live in a world that is cursed by sin; it is now groaning and travailing in pain, but it is to be delivered. Someday it is to be redeemed, and sin is to be removed.

A little later in this chapter we are told that even heaven itself had to be cleansed (see v. 23). Someone says, "My gracious, is it dirty in heaven?" Yes, that is where sin originated, where Lucifer led his rebellion. Therefore, Christ's sacrifice was adequate and it was complete. It was a finished transaction that covered all of God's creation which has been touched by sin.

> Were the whole realm of nature mine,
> That were a present far too small;
> Love so amazing, so divine,
> Demands my soul, my life, my all.
>   "When I Survey the Wondrous Cross"
>   —Isaac Watts

The ashes of the heifer were to be kept in a clean place and then mixed with water when they were used. I think that the water speaks of the Word of God. It is the Word of God which reveals sin in the life of the believer.

The sacrifice of Christ provided redemption for the future—for your redemption and my redemption. It also provided redemption for the sins of those in the Old Testament. The Old Testament saints were saved by faith—Abraham was saved by faith. How? He believed God and brought a lamb. Was that lamb adequate? No; it prefigured Christ. The sacrifice of Christ looks forward and it looks backward.

> **How much more shall the blood of Christ, who through the eternal Spirit offered himself without spot to God, purge your conscience from dead works to serve the living God? [Heb. 9:14].**

If the blood of animals could remove ceremonial defilement, surely the blood of Christ can take away the guilt of sin. After all, if the blood of bulls and goats had been adequate, Christ never would have shed His blood to do the adequate job.

"Purge your conscience." The ordinance of the red heifer in Numbers 19 speaks of the life of the believer and the fact that as believers you and I need constant cleansing. "But if we walk in the light, we have fellowship one with another, and the blood of Jesus Christ his Son cleanseth [keeps on cleansing] us from all sin. . . . If we confess our sins, he is faithful and just to forgive us our sins, and to cleanse us from all unrighteousness" (1 John 1:7,9). You see, the blood of Christ cleanses, not the flesh, but the conscience.

It is the conscience of man that needs to be cleansed. You and I have not really arrived until we enter into this marvelous sacrifice of Christ, recognizing His authority to absolutely forgive and cleanse us from sin. It is the conscience that has been made alert by the Word of God, but it can also rest in a finished salvation. We can pillow our heads at night knowing that our sins are entirely, totally, fully forgiven. We can know that we are right with God because Christ has made it right.

I heard a story of a man who had a little boy who did something wrong and went to his father to ask him to forgive him. The father told the little boy he would, and said, "Because you have come and confessed it, I will forgive you." But the little boy came again and asked forgiveness. The father said, "Sure. I've already forgiven you." The little boy kept coming back and coming back and coming back. Finally, the father said, "Son, I'm going to paddle you, if you don't quit coming to me! I told you I'd forgiven you."

How many times do we find believers who say, "Oh, I'm not sure I'm saved. I'm not sure I'm saved." And they keep going to the Lord. My friend, I think He would say, "I've already forgiven you. If you trust in My Son, your sins are forgiven." We need to enter into that and rest upon His Word.

"Purge your conscience *from dead works.*" Dead works have to do with works that you do thinking they will save you. You see, we are dead in trespasses and sins, and all that a dead person can do is dead works. I have never heard of a dead person doing live work—it just can't be done. Anything that you do to try to earn your salvation is a dead work.

Because good works are never a cause of salvation but are a result of salvation, the writer goes on to say, "purge your conscience from dead works *to serve the living God.*" The word *serve* is actually *worship*—"to worship the living God." Worship and service go together. You can't serve God without worshipping Him; neither can you worship Him without serving Him. When I see a lazy saint doing nothing for God, I don't question his salvation, but I do question his worship. Does he really worship God? Oh, if you fall down before Him in adoration and praise, then you are going to get up on your feet to start doing something for Him, my friend.

I had this bit of verse written in the first Bible I ever owned, which my mother had given to me:

> I do not work my soul to save—
> That work my Lord has done.
> But I will work like any slave
> For love of God's dear Son.
> —Author unknown

**And for this cause he is the mediator of the new testa-
ment, that by means of death, for the redemption of the
transgressions that were under the first testament, they
which are called might receive the promise of eternal
inheritance [Heb. 9:15].**

"And for this cause he is the mediator of the new testament [or, cove-
nant]." The emphasis is upon the fact that He is the mediator of the
New Covenant. Those who came under the old covenant, the Old Testament saints, were saved because they were looking forward to His coming when they brought their sacrifices. I do not know how much they
understood, and yet the Lord Jesus said, "Your father Abraham rejoiced to see my day: and he saw it, and was glad" (John 8:56). Genesis
doesn't tell us that; the Lord Jesus did. I believe that all of the Old
Testament worthies looked forward to the coming of Christ. In other
words, God saved on credit. The blood of bulls and goats never took
away their sins. They brought the sacrifices by faith, and when Christ
came, He died ". . . for the remission of sins that are past . . ." (Rom.
3:25); that is, He died for the sins of all from Adam right down to the
time of the cross. And since then, you and I also come to Him by faith.

**For where a testament is, there must also of necessity be
the death of the testator.**

**For a testament is of force after men are dead: otherwise
it is of no strength at all while the testator liveth [Heb.
9:16–17].**

"Testament" could be translated *will*. If you have made a will and you
are still alive, your will does nothing for anyone. It doesn't operate
until you die. Now the reference here is to a will that was made by a
man who died. He couldn't save anyone as long as He lived. Don't
misunderstand me—what I am saying is that the *life* of Christ could
never save you. It is the *death* of Christ which saves you.

**Whereupon neither the first testament was dedicated
without blood.**

> For when Moses had spoken every precept to all the peo-
> ple according to the law, he took the blood of calves and
> of goats, with water, and scarlet wool, and hyssop, and
> sprinkled both the book, and all the people.
>
> Saying, This is the blood of the testament which God
> hath enjoined unto you.
>
> Moreover he sprinkled with blood both the tabernacle,
> and all the vessels of the ministry.
>
> And almost all things are by the law purged with blood;
> and without shedding of blood is no remission [Heb.
> 9:18–22].

The word *blood* occurs in this section six times, revealing the place and the power of the blood in the Old Testament ritual. "Without shedding of blood is no remission" is the axiom of the Old Testament. Also the blood is very important in the New Testament. As the hymn writer put it, "there is power in the blood of the Lamb." In Revelation we find that the victory was won through the blood of the Lamb, not through some individual's ingenuity, or physical strength, or even spiritual strength.

> It was therefore necessary that the patterns of things in
> the heavens should be purified with these; but the heav-
> enly things themselves with better sacrifices than these
> [Heb. 9:23].

These heavenly things needed cleansing because sin originated in heaven (see v. 11). The blood of bulls and goats has never been shed in heaven—there is no denying that that would be crude. However, the blood of Christ, we believe, is in heaven, and that is not crude at all.

> For Christ is not entered into the holy places made with
> hands, which are the figures of the true; but into heaven
> itself, now to appear in the presence of God for us [Heb.
> 9:24].

The tabernacle on earth was just a figure—the reality is in heaven. "Now to appear in the *presence* of God for us" means before the very face of God. Christ has not entered into a manmade sanctuary. It is spiritual but real. He died on earth to save us. He lives in heaven to keep us saved. He is there for us.

> **Nor yet that he should offer himself often, as the high priest entereth into the holy place every year with blood of others [Heb. 9:25].**

The high priest entered the earthly tabernacle with blood not his own, and he entered often.

> **For then must he often have suffered since the foundation of the world: but now once in the end of the world hath he appeared to put away sin by the sacrifice of himself [Heb. 9:26].**

"But now once in the end of the world" should read "the end of the *age*." This has no reference to what some people call the end of the world. Actually, the Bible does not teach the end of the world; it does teach the end of the age.

"Hath he appeared to put away sin by the sacrifice of himself." Christ came, made under the Law. He appeared at the end of the Law age, and He instituted a new age, the age of grace.

> **And as it is appointed unto men once to die, but after this the judgment [Heb. 9:27].**

Death is in the natural sequence of events for man. For the unsaved man, after death there is nothing but judgment. If the death of Christ does not save you, there is nothing ahead of you but judgment.

Death is not appointed unto *all* men—thank God for that. It is appointed unto men once to die, but some are not going to die. I hear people talk today about old age and, oh, how they want to die and get into the presence of the Lord. I don't know about you, but I don't mind waiting. I'm in no hurry to die! I hope I can live until He comes. I don't know whether I will, but that is the way I would like it.

> Oh joy! oh delight! should we go without dying,
> No sickness, no sadness, no dread and no crying.
> Caught up through the clouds with our Lord into glory,
> When Jesus receives "His own."
> O Lord Jesus, how long, how long
> Ere we shout the glad song, Christ returneth!
> Hallelujah! hallelujah! Amen, Hallelujah! Amen.
> > "Christ Returneth"
> > —H. L. Turner

These words by H. L. Turner in "Christ Returneth" express the thoughts we cherish about His coming.

So Christ was once offered to bear the sins of many; and unto them that look for him shall he appear the second time without sin unto salvation [Heb. 9:28].

This is not speaking of the Rapture, but of His coming as sovereign to judge the earth. (However, believers will not come into judgment.) When He appears the second time it will not be to settle the sin question. He is not going to come the next time to walk around the Sea of Galilee or through the streets of Jerusalem to see what men will do with His sacrifice. He is coming in judgment.

Therefore today we can put it very simply: there is just one of two places for your sin—either your sin is on you, or it is on Christ. If you have not accepted the sacrifice of Christ, if you are not trusting Him as your redeemer, if He is no authority to you, then there is nothing ahead of you but the judgment of the Great White Throne. No one who appears there is going to be saved, but everyone will be given a fair chance to present their works and discover that God was right all along. And I have news for you: God is always right. So today if your sin is on you, there is nothing that can remove it but the death of Christ.

When Christ comes the next time it will be "without sin unto salvation"—that is, He will *complete* salvation at that time. Our salvation is in three tenses: I have been saved; I am being saved; I shall be saved. "Beloved, now are we the sons of God, and it doth not yet appear what we shall be: but we know that, when he shall appear, we shall be like him; for we shall see him as he is" (1 John 3:2). Now that is going to be a great day. It is going to be a great day for Vernon McGee, so don't you be dissatisfied with me, will you not? God is not through with me.

Down in Mississippi a dear little lady wearing a sunbonnet got up in a testimony meeting under the brush arbor and said, "Most Christians ought to have written on their backs, 'This is not the best that the grace of God can do.'" Well, that should be written on the backs of *all* Christians. God is not through with any of us. Thank God for that! He is going to appear the second time without sin unto *salvation*—He is going to deliver us. But, my friend, He will not come to settle the sin question for anyone who has not accepted Him—to them He is coming as judge.

CHAPTER 10

Without a chapter break, the writer of this epistle continues with the subject of the superior sacrifice.

> **For the law having a shadow of good things to come, and not the very image of the things, can never with those sacrifices which they offered year by year continually make the comers thereunto perfect [Heb. 10:1].**

As he concluded chapter 9 the writer said that if Christ had failed to save in His death at His first coming, there would be nothing afterward but *judgment*. My friend, if you reject Jesus Christ as Savior, you will have the saddest funeral possible. I have conducted many funerals, and some of them were for unsaved people. There is no sorrow like that of a funeral in a family of unsaved people—and that's the way it should be. I recall one instance in which a wife, who was almost an alcoholic, had lost her husband. She had leaned on him a great deal. I tried to give a message, not of comfort, but of good news, presenting the Gospel. Afterward she came to me, looked into my face and asked, "Is there any hope at all?" I said, "Well, there is a hope for *you*." There was no hope for him whatsoever. He was a blasphemer, and he had told me that he had no use for the church; he had no use for Jesus Christ; he had no use for anything Christian. There was nothing ahead for him but judgment.

Beginning with this word *for* the writer continues the theme of Christ's sacrifice for sin.

"For the law having a shadow of good things to come, and not the very image of the things." The Mosaic Law served a good purpose in that it was a picture which *taught* Israel. Because God had taught Israel so thoroughly, He judged the nation severely. When the Lord Jesus was there in the flesh He said, ". . . how often would I have gathered thy children together, as a hen doth gather her brood under her wings,

and ye would not!" (Luke 13:34). My friend, if you don't believe that
God's judgment was really a severe one, go to Jerusalem and walk
around the streets of old Jerusalem. Walk in the area where we know
Jesus moved. All of it is covered over with debris today. Why? Because
the city has been judged. Oh, how often the Lord had attempted to
gather His chosen people to Himself! He had given them the Old Testament with the clear teaching of the tabernacle ritual.

Contrast the light that they had to the darkness in which my ancestors lived way up there in Germany. Boy, were they pagan and heathen
in those days! And my ancestors over in Scotland were dirty and filthy.
Then the Gospel came to them, and, thank God, some of them trusted
Christ. I had a grandfather on my father's side who apparently was a
godly man. I am thankful for the men who carried the Gospel to Eu-
rope. That gave the Gentiles a break, you see.

But the nation of Israel had the Old Testament, which was (and still
is) a picture book, a book of ABCs. That is the reason so many folk
miss its meaning. When theologians come to it, they have to find
something profound in it. But it is a simple picture book in which God
is trying to tell all of us little children down here that He died for us. It
is just as simple as that, my friend.

Now let me call your attention to another thing that is very important. Notice that the Law had to do with the tabernacle and the sacrifices. This idea that you can separate God's commandments from His
ceremonial law is entirely wrong. If you want to return to the legal
system and put yourself under the Ten Commandments, you had better
build a little tabernacle for yourself and start raising goats and sheep,
because you are going to need them. But, my friend, Christ finished
all of that. We now are on a different basis, a higher plane altogether.
For instance, God wants to bring *joy* into your life. The Law never
promised joy. There was thunder and lightning, and people were smit-
ten dead at the giving of the Law. But when Jesus came, it was *He* who
died that we might have life.

**For then would they not have ceased to be offered? be-
cause that the worshippers once purged should have
had no more conscience of sins [Heb. 10:2].**

"For then would they not have ceased to be offered?" If the sacrifice they offered could have taken away their guilt, one sacrifice would have been enough.

It is very interesting to note that after the Lord Jesus died, it was only a few years until the temple was destroyed. And Israel has not been able to put up another temple. Oh, they have a little miniature temple for display over on the new side of Jerusalem at the Holy City Hotel, but they don't have a temple today. It doesn't look as if they will get one soon either. You see, when Christ became the sacrifice, that ended the need for the tabernacle and temple.

Today Israel is not offering sacrifices. I spoke to a very delightful Jewish guide in Jerusalem. His hair was as gray as it could be. He said that it had turned gray when he was only nineteen years of age after he had heard that his father and mother, sisters and brothers had been killed in Russia. He was a delightful fellow, and he took me around to show me the model of the temple at the hotel I mentioned. As we were looking at it, I asked him (although perhaps I should not have), "Where is the brazen altar?" He looked at me with surprise and said, "Oh, we have come past that. Today we have an *ethical* religion." Well, a lot of folk have an ethical religion, but, my friend, that bloody sacrifice was necessary that the human family might have forgiveness of sins.

"For then would they not have ceased to be offered? because that the worshippers once purged should have had no more conscience of sins." They would no longer have any feelings of guilt or consciousness of sin.

But in those sacrifices there is a remembrance again made of sins every year [Heb. 10:3].

So, actually, what those sacrifices did was to remind the Israelite that the sacrificial system was not complete—or they wouldn't have to come back and repeat it every day. The sacrifices were only a shadow, *skian* in the Greek, meaning "a hazy outline." The old sacrifices were shadow, never substance. And, my friend, shadows are not enough. You can't live in the shadow of a house; you need a house.

Again, the sacrifices would not have had to be repeated if they had been complete. For instance, when a man says that he is cured of disease and yet he is still taking medicine every hour, that man is not cured. And when a man keeps bringing sacrifices every year, that man is not cured of sin. It is Christ who made the one sacrifice once and for all. In those sacrifices there was a reminder of sins year by year. Here they go through the great Day of Atonement every year. What did it mean? The answer had not arrived until yonder on Golgotha when Jesus cried out, *"Tetelestai!"* Finished! My friend, then it was finished. And the next year there was no need for a Day of Atonement. In fact, he will tell us that to go through a sacrifice today is to tread underfoot the blood of Jesus.

> **For it is not possible that the blood of bulls and of goats should take away sins [Heb. 10:4].**

The blood of the animal sacrifices only covered over the sins until the Lamb of God would come to take away the sin of the world (see John 1:29).

Now here is a tremendous passage—

> **Wherefore when he cometh into the world, he saith, Sacrifice and offering thou wouldest not, but a body hast thou prepared me:**
>
> **In burnt offerings and sacrifices for sin thou hast had no pleasure.**
>
> **Then said I, Lo, I come (in the volume of the book it is written to me,) to do thy will, O God.**
>
> **Above when he said, Sacrifice and offering and burnt offerings and offering for sin thou wouldest not, neither hadst pleasure therein; which are offered by the law;**
>
> **Then said he, Lo, I come to do thy will, O God. He taketh away the first, that he may establish the second.**
>
> **By the which will we are sanctified through the offering of the body of Jesus Christ once for all [Heb. 10:5–10].**

I want to insert a cross reference here to make this section of the Word of God very meaningful to you. Going back to the Book of Exodus, we find in chapter 19 the preparation for the giving of the Mosaic Law, and in chapter 20 the giving of the Ten Commandments. After that, God makes a gracious provision by the sacrificial system. You see, the altar goes right along with the Law. Then in chapter 21 we come upon something that seems very much out of place. It is one of the most beautiful references in the Bible. The Law has been given, and now God says to Moses: "Now these are the judgments which thou shalt set before them. If thou buy an Hebrew servant, six years he shall serve: and in the seventh he shall go out free for nothing. [They couldn't have a slave of their own people more than six years.] If he came in by himself, he shall go out by himself: if he were married, then his wife shall go out with him. If his master have given him a wife, and she have born him sons or daughters; the wife and her children shall be her master's, and he shall go out by himself. And if the servant shall plainly say, I love my master, my wife, and my children; I will not go out free: Then his master shall bring him unto the judges; he shall also bring him to the door, or unto the door post; and his master shall bore his ear through with an awl [the lobe of the ear would be pierced]; and he shall serve him for ever." (Exod. 21:1-6).

In that day if you saw a man walking along with a hole in his ear, you would know that he had been given a wife, and that he had paid the price of permanent servitude for her. It was a tremendous law and certainly a lovely thing, but what is the meaning of it?

Well, let's follow the meaning of it. In Psalm 40:6-7 we read, "Sacrifice and offering thou didst not desire; mine ears hast thou opened [that is, pierced with an awl]: burnt offering and sin offering hast thou not required. Then said I, Lo, I come: in the volume of the book it is written of me." This is quoted in the Book of Hebrews and applied to the Lord Jesus Christ. Here is one of the most beautiful pictures in Scripture. The Lord Jesus came to this earth, grew to manhood, and at thirty years of age He began His earthly ministry. When He came to the end of that ministry, He could say, "Which of you convicteth me of sin?" (see John 8:46). He was holy, harmless, undefiled, and separate from sinners. He could have stepped off this earth any day that He wanted to, gone back to heaven and left this earth in sin—left you and me in the slavery of sin. But He loved us, and God so loved the world that He gave His only begotten Son. So instead of His ear being pierced with an awl, He was given a body. A body for what? For death—to die on the cross. "By the which will we are sanctified through the offering of the body of Jesus Christ once for all" (Heb. 10:10). Referring to that law in Exodus, if a master gave his slave a woman to marry, and he loved her, he could choose to stay in slavery with her. In like manner the Lord Jesus Christ has been given the body of believers which we call the church as His bride. In His prayer in John 17:9 the Lord said to His Father concerning them, "They are mine. You gave them to Me." The Lord loves us; He paid the price for us. But the interesting thing is that He didn't stay in slavery; He went back to the right hand of the Majesty on high, and some day He is going to take us out of the slavery of sin to be with Him. He alone could do that. How wonderful this is!

> There is a green hill, far away,
> Without a city wall.
> Where the dear Lord was crucified,
> Who died to save us all.
>
> There was no other good enough,
> To pay the price of sin.
> He only could unlock the gate
> Of heaven to let us in.
>   "There is a Green Hill Far Away"
>   —Mrs. Cecil F. Alexander

What a beautiful picture of Christ this section of Scripture gives us!

And every priest standeth daily ministering and offering oftentimes the same sacrifices, which can never take away sins [Heb. 10:11].

The offerings could only cover the sin; they were an atonement, but they could never take away sins. The offerings were just a reminder

that men were sinners and that the sin question had not yet been settled.

**But this man, after he had offered one sacrifice for sins
for ever, sat down on the right hand of God [Heb. 10:12].**

Why did He sit down? Was He tired? No. Did He sit down because He
did not want to do anything? No. Jesus sat down because His work was
finished—"*one* sacrifice for sins *for ever.*"

**From henceforth expecting till his enemies be made his
footstool [Heb. 10:13].**

Our Lord is just waiting. There are a few more people to be saved. We
pray, "O come now, Lord Jesus," but He says, "No, not yet. We are
going to wait, because I want to save some more." He is giving you an
opportunity, friend, if you are not saved. Psalm 110:1 says, "The LORD
said unto my Lord, Sit thou at my right hand, until I make thine enemies thy footstool," referring to the second coming of Christ to the
earth. But in the meantime He is waiting for more of the human family
to come to Him.

**For by one offering he hath perfected for ever them that
are sanctified [Heb. 10:14].**

One offering does what many offerings could not do. If *Christ* cannot
save you and keep you, then God has no other way to save you and keep
you.

**Whereof the Holy Ghost also is a witness to us: for after
that he had said before,**

**This is the covenant that I will make with them after
those days, saith the Lord, I will put my laws into their
hearts, and in their minds will I write them;**

**And their sins and iniquities will I remember no more
[Heb. 10:15–17].**

This is the essential part of the quotation from Jeremiah 31. God says, "I'm going to make a new covenant with Israel." God is not through with them. If you will read your Bible you will see that.

Now let me remind you that in this section of Hebrews we are seeing the greatest division in the Word of God. It is like a Grand Canyon which is placed between the old covenant and the New Covenant, the Old Testament and the New Testament. And let's remember that God gave both of them. Referring to verse 9, notice that it says, "He taketh away the first, that he may establish the second." He taketh away the first (that is, the first covenant), that He may establish the second covenant. When the Lord Jesus died upon the cross, something very important happened: the veil was rent in twain. No longer are men to come to God through the sacrifice of the blood of bulls and goats; now the Lord Jesus has made a way for us through His own body—a way for you and me. Notice again verse 10: "By the which will we are sanctified through the offering of the body of Jesus Christ once." In the Authorized Version the two words *for all* that conclude this verse are in italics, meaning they were supplied by the translators. The verse is more accurate without them, because the emphasis is on the fact that Christ did it one time so that sacrifices are to end. It is interesting that ever since the destruction of the temple in A.D. 70 by Titus the Roman, there has been no bloody sacrifice offered in Jerusalem. There are no blood sacrifices being offered there today, and the prospects for them being offered in the near future are very dim. Christ took away the first that He might establish the second.

The importance of this cannot be overemphasized. You see, in the first covenant were many rules and regulations. The old covenant was a law, a law that had a great many details. There was the ceremonial law with many details in regard to the sacrifices; there were the Ten Commandments and other commandments or rules. Actually rules and regulations appeal to human nature. Men feel that it is easy to obey rules, which is the reason so many folk today will tell you that the Sermon on the Mount is their religion. They may not know exactly what it says or what it means, but they like it because it has rules, which they kid themselves into believing they can follow. The whole history of mankind and the multitude of cults and "isms" springing up in our day demonstrate that this is true. Man likes to live by certain rules and follow certain rituals.

Now in the New Covenant we are under an altogether different system. Paul had mentioned to the Corinthian believers: "Who also hath made us able ministers of the new testament [the New Covenant]; not of the letter, but of the spirit: for the letter killeth, but the spirit giveth life" (2 Cor. 3:6). Some strange individuals have come up with the novel interpretation that this verse means they should not study the Bible! They say that "the letter" means the Bible and it is the Spirit that gives life. Well, of course that is not what Paul is saying, as the following verse makes clear. "But if the ministration of death, written and engraven in stones, was glorious. . . ." Obviously, this refers to the Ten Commandments, so now we know that the "letter" is the commandments. The Ten Commandments were the ministration of death. My friend, the Law *kills*. The Law never saved anyone. It will kill you because it brings you under the judgment of God. It is the Spirit who gives life, and you and I are living in this day when the Holy Spirit is the one who regenerates us, who leads us, and who shows us the will of God.

> **Now where remission of these is, there is no more offering for sin [Heb. 10:18].**

"Now"—the sacrificial system began with Abel and ended with the death of Christ. This verse concludes the doctrinal section.

ENCOURAGEMENT

Hebrews 10:19–25 is the practical section of this chapter, and it speaks of privilege and responsibility.

> **Having therefore, brethren, boldness to enter into the holiest by the blood of Jesus [Heb. 10:19].**

"Boldness" is boldness of speech; it has no thought of arrogance. Now notice this carefully—how do we get into the holiest, that is, into God's presence? By the blood of Jesus.

By a new and living way, which he hath consecrated for us, through the veil, that is to say, his flesh [Heb. 10:20].

That veil was torn in two when Christ was crucified on the cross, which indicated that the way to God was open.

"Through the veil, that is to say, his flesh"—*flesh* is the same word we find in the prologue of John's gospel where he said that "the Word became flesh." John didn't say that it was a new and living way open to God, because the Incarnation, the *life* of Christ saves no one. We enter into the holiest by the *blood* of Jesus. Our right of entrance is not through His incarnation but through the rending of the veil; that is, through His death. You and I have the privilege of worshipping God, not because of the *life* of Jesus, but because of His *death* for us upon the cross. Oh, my friend, this distinction is so important!

"By a new and living way." The word *new* is from the Greek word *prosphatos*, meaning "newly slain." It speaks of the fact that the Lord Jesus Christ has opened up for you and me a new and living way to God through His crucifixion, through His death upon the cross. The old sacrifices won't help you anymore, friend.

And having an high priest over the house of God [Heb. 10:21].

What a wonderful privilege to have an advocate with the Father, Jesus Christ, the righteous, who always lives to make intercession for us.

"Through the veil"—when Christ dismissed His spirit as He hung there upon the cross, the veil of the temple was torn in two, which opened the way into the very presence of the Father.

Now we have an invitation. Some expositors believe it is directed to the unsaved. I believe it is both to the unsaved and to the saved. Since we have an High Priest at the right hand of God—

Let us draw near with a true heart in full assurance of faith, having our hearts sprinkled from an evil conscience, and our bodies washed with pure water [Heb. 10:22].

This has to do with the dedication of priests in the Aaronic priesthood. Moses sprinkled them with the water of dedication. And they had to be washed, denoting that they were set aside for the service of God. In like manner our dedication to God enables us to draw near with a true heart.

"In full assurance of faith," or in fullness of faith, has nothing to do with the amount of our faith; it has everything to do with the *object* of our faith. Real faith always depends on the object of faith. You see, faith can be misplaced—you can put your faith in some individual on earth and be disappointed. Faith is not just believing that there is a God—all that means is that you are not an atheist. Not only should you have a knowledge of God and know the way of righteousness, but you should act upon your faith. Real faith means that you have really received the Lord Jesus Christ as your personal Savior. That has been made very clear to us. In John 1:11–12 we read, "He came unto his own, and his own received him not. But as many as received him, to them gave he power [the authority] to become the sons of God, even to them that [do no more or less than] believe on his name." Faith in Christ means to *receive* Christ as Savior. Faith is action based on knowledge. God never asks us to take a leap in the dark. I disagree with the theologian who said, "Faith is to leap in the dark." If this is true, don't leap, because you may find yourself going off a ten-story building! You don't need to leap in the dark, because God has given us knowledge. "So then faith cometh by hearing, and hearing by the word of God" (Rom. 10:17). God has put down a foundation for our faith. "For other foundation can no man lay than that is laid, which is Jesus Christ" (1 Cor. 3:11). You get on the foundation, friend. That's knowledge, but it is faith that puts you there. Faith is action that is based on knowledge, which means to trust Christ personally as your Savior.

"Let us draw near with a true heart in full assurance of faith, having our hearts sprinkled from an evil conscience, and our bodies washed with pure water." This means that you and I as believers are members of a priesthood. One of the great truths that John Calvin recovered was the priesthood of all believers. Every believer is a priest, and, as such, you can come to God with boldness of speech. So many people ask the preacher to pray for them, which is all right, but we need to remember that *all* believers have access to God. You have as much right in God's presence as I have, or as anyone else has, because we come by this "newly sacrificed" way that Christ has made for us. It is on that basis that we come to God.

Let us hold fast the profession of our faith without wavering; (for he is faithful that promised;) [Heb. 10:23].

"Let us hold fast the profession of our faith." Actually, "faith" has in it the thought of hope. Let us draw near to God, but let us hold fast to our confession of faith. Why? Because we have a hope, and hope is for the future, you see. How wonderful it is that we can come near to God in the full assurance of faith, and also that we can hold fast the confession of our faith because we have a hope. As the hymn writer has put it,

> So near, so very near to God,
>   We cannot nearer be;
> For in the Person of His Son,
>   We are as near as He.

> So dear, so very dear to God,
>   We cannot dearer be,
> For in the Person of His Son,
>   We are as dear as He.
>   —Author unknown

We are to draw near (v. 22). We are to hold fast (v. 23). And now a third thing:

And let us consider one another to provoke unto love and to good works [Heb. 10:24].

"Let us consider one another to provoke"—"provoke" is from the Greek word *paroxusmos*, from which we get our English word *paroxysm*, which literally means "with a view to excitement." Let us consider one another to provoke unto love and to good works.

Do I annoy you? Some Christians tell me that I have troubled their consciences. Well, I hope I have troubled your conscience so that you will love one another and so that you will do some good works for God.

Not forsaking the assembling of ourselves together, as the manner of some is; but exhorting one another: and so much the more, as ye see the day approaching [Heb. 10:25].

If there ever was a time when believers needed to come together, it is today. Instead of chopping down each other, we need to draw together in love around the person of Christ.

"Exhorting one another." We need to study the Word of God together. God has something for a group that He will not give to any one individual. One of the reasons I like to teach the Word of God is selfish. It is because God won't let me grow in the knowledge of His Word unless I share it. We are not to forsake the assembling of ourselves together. If you have a Bible study at your church, be sure to go because there is a blessing for you there that you can't get when you study the Bible by yourself. So these are the three "let us" verses:

> Draw near in faith (toward God)
> Draw near in hope (for ourselves)
> Draw near in love (for others)

This presents again the three graces: faith, hope, and love. How practical this epistle is!

"As ye see the day approaching." To the Jewish people who are being addressed in this epistle, "the day approaching" probably meant the day when their temple would be destroyed, which it was in A.D. 70. Remember that the believers were meeting together in the temple. That is where they were on the Day of Pentecost when the Holy Spirit came. Peter and John were going into the temple when they met the lame man at the beautiful gate. But where will they gather together after the temple is destroyed? The writer is urging them, "As you see the day approaching when you won't have a meeting place, just keep meeting together." And the church started by meeting in private homes, by the way.

DANGER SIGNAL: THE PERIL OF DESPISING

This is the most solemn warning of all. In fact, it makes your hair stand on end!

For if we sin wilfully after that we have received the knowledge of the truth, there remaineth no more sacrifice for sins [Heb. 10:26].

It is a fearful thing to fall into the hands of the living God! Simon Peter said, "For it had been better for them not to have known the way of righteousness, than, after they have known it, to turn from the holy commandment delivered unto them" (2 Pet. 2:21). The warning is to the Hebrew believers because many of them were continuing to go to the temple and some were actually offering sacrifices there. They were keeping up a front, pretending that they were still under the Mosaic Law. In so doing they also were making it clear that the sacrifice of Christ was meaningless to them. Since the animal sacrifices prefigured Christ's sacrifice, now that Christ had died on the cross, all of that was fulfilled. Therefore, what before had been done in obedience to God's command, now has become willful sin. To continue to offer blood sacrifices which had been fulfilled by Christ was a frightful, terrible thing. They were acting as if the temple sacrifices were going on forever. The writer to the Hebrews is telling them that they cannot look to the temple any more, because there is no longer a sacrifice for sin. If a person rejects the truth of Christ's death for sin, there is no other sacrifice for sin available, and there is no other way to come to God. They are to look to Christ now rather than to the temple. If they refuse to do this, there is nothing left for them but judgment. The Word of God is very expressive in this connection.

"If we sin wilfully after that we have received the knowledge of the truth." This means to go on sinning willfully by offering the sacrifices. It is an attitude toward the Word of God which God calls willful rebellion. There is no more sacrifice in the Old Testament or the New Testament for presumptuous sins.

> **But a certain fearful looking for of judgment and fiery indignation, which shall devour the adversaries [Heb. 10:27].**

If the death of Christ over nineteen hundred years ago was not adequate, then *nothing* is adequate. God is not going to do something else to redeem us. Christ is not going to die again—and, of course, it is not necessary for Him to do so. It becomes willful disobedience on the part of those who "have received the knowledge of the truth" to continue with the temple ritual and offering of sacrifices.

Now he will make a comparison.

> **He that despised Moses' law died without mercy under two or three witnesses [Heb. 10:28].**

Now note the comparison—

> **Of how much sorer punishment, suppose ye, shall he be thought worthy, who hath trodden under foot the Son of God, and hath counted the blood of the covenant, wherewith he was sanctified, an unholy thing, and hath done despite unto the Spirit of grace? [Heb. 10:29].**

This is probably the most solemn statement in the Word of God.

"Wherewith he was sanctified" refers to Christ, the Son of God. They crucified "to themselves the Son of God afresh" (Heb. 6:6). To act as if the death of Christ is inadequate to settle the sin question, and to go on as if He had not died, is to treat the blood of Christ as something you despise. Knowledge creates responsibility. If, after you have heard the Gospel, you turn your back on Jesus Christ—my friend, someone ought to tell you that you are going to *hell!* This is not what *I* say; it is what *God* says.

**For we know him that hath said, Vengeance belongeth
unto me, I will recompense, saith the Lord. And again,
The Lord shall judge his people [Heb. 10:30].**

Friend, God is going to judge. He is the sovereign ruler of this universe. We are all going to have to appear before Him. God has a sovereign right to judge, which He has not surrendered. "For the time is come that judgment must begin at the house of God: and if it first begin at us, what shall the end be of them that obey not the gospel of God? And if the righteous scarcely be saved, where shall the ungodly and the sinner appear?" (1 Pet. 4:17–18).

**It is a fearful thing to fall into the hands of the living
God [Heb. 10:31].**

This is a very interesting verse, and it will be profitable to spend a little time with it. This verse is for Christians and unbelievers also. It *is* a fearful thing to fall into the hands of the living God! In Ezra 7:9 we read, "For upon the first day of the first month began he [Ezra] to go up from Babylon, and on the first day of the fifth month came he to Jerusalem, according to the good hand of his God upon him." In this verse the hand of God is upon this man for *good*. And God wants to put His hand upon you for good, but sometimes He puts a very *heavy* hand upon His children. He chastens them—or, as we say, He takes them to the woodshed. I have been to the woodshed. Maybe you have been there, too. David had been there, and in Psalm 32:4 he says, "For day and night thy hand was heavy upon me: my moisture is turned into the drought of summer. Selah." What was God doing? He was chastening David. He had taken him to the woodshed. David tried to cover up his sin, but God forced him to confess it and deal with it. For a similar reason sometimes God's heavy hand is upon us who are His children.

However, God's hand of chastening is altogether different from His hand of judgment. He says, "Vengeance belongeth unto me. I will recompense." God does not take vengeance in a spiteful or vindictive manner. But God is going to *judge* sin, and that is something that needs to be emphasized in our day. Listen again to the psalmist: "For in the hand of the LORD there is a cup, and the wine is red; it is full of mixture; and he poureth out of the same: but the dregs thereof, all the wicked of the earth shall wring them out, and drink them" (Ps. 75:8). You see, the psalmist as well as the prophet spoke of judgment as a time coming when the cup of wrath will be filled up. And it is filling up today. God is in no hurry to move; He is longsuffering, not willing that any should perish, but that cup of judgment is filling up. And, my friend, it is a bitter cup.

This cup of God's judgment is ahead of everyone "who hath trodden under foot the Son of God, and hath counted the blood of the covenant, wherewith he was sanctified, an unholy thing, and hath done despite unto the Spirit of grace." My friend, if you despise what Christ has done for you on the cross, there is nothing ahead of you but judgment. You have no hope whatsoever.

This is the same point the writer is making to these Hebrew believers. Under the Mosaic Law they could bring a sacrifice every year—or any day if they wanted to. But they cannot do that any longer; that is over. Now they have to turn (even as we do) to the Lord Jesus Christ.

Now the writer gives a personal word to these Jewish folk to whom he is writing:

> **But call to remembrance the former days, in which, after ye were illuminated, ye endured a great fight of afflictions [Heb. 10:32].**

I assume that the Hebrews to whom this epistle was written were saved. There seems to be no question in the writer's mind about their being believers.

> **Partly, whilst ye were made a gazingstock both by reproaches and afflictions; and partly, whilst ye became companions of them that were so used.**
>
> **For ye had compassion of me in my bonds, and took joyfully the spoiling of your goods, knowing in yourselves that ye have in heaven a better and an enduring substance [Heb. 10:33–34].**

"Partly, whilst ye were made a gazingstock." The Christians were made a public spectacle.

"And took joyfully the spoiling of your goods." Apparently some of the believers had been imprisoned for their faith while others had experienced the seizure of their possessions. The writer is reminding them of their faith and patience during this trying time.

Cast not away therefore your confidence, which hath great recompense of reward [Heb. 10:35].

"Cast not away therefore your confidence" is another way of saying "let us hold fast the confession of our faith without wavering."

For ye have need of patience, that, after ye have done the will of God, ye might receive the promise [Heb. 10:36].

Patience and faith are wedded in Scripture. After exercising faith in the midst of trials, then they are to display patience with the future hope of the fulfillment of faith.

For yet a little while, and he that shall come will come, and will not tarry [Heb. 10:37].

I hear the expression many times, "I'll see you next time, Dr. McGee, if the Lord tarry." I've got news for people who say that. The Lord is not going to tarry. Some folks acts as though He keeps putting off His coming, that He is tarrying. He is not going to tarry. It is on His calendar to come. Somebody asks, "When is He coming?" Well, the Lord won't let me see His calendar; so I don't know. I hear some folk talk as if they have seen His calendar, but I think they have been looking at man's calendar, because nobody has seen God's calendar. However, we can be sure that Christ will come on the day appointed; it is as certain as His first coming to this earth.

Now the just shall live by faith: but if any man draw back, my soul shall have no pleasure in him [Heb. 10:38].

This verse is a quotation from Habakkuk 2:3–4, quoted also in Romans and in Galatians. It is an important verse. Each epistle that quotes this verse puts a different emphasis on it. In the Epistle to the Romans the emphasis is upon "the *just* shall live by faith"—how God justifies the sinner. Here in the Epistle to the Hebrews, the emphasis is upon "the just shall *live* by faith." There have been several references to the *living* God, and this epistle tells of a *living* intercessor. He is the same one who died on the cross for us and came back from the dead. The emphasis is upon His resurrection and His being the living Christ at God's right hand. Therefore since we who are His own have a living God and a living Savior at God's right hand, we shall *live* by faith. As I have said before, our faith is not a leap in the dark. It rests upon the Word of God. The just shall *live* by faith. Now in the Epistle to the Galatians Paul emphasizes faith; the just shall live by *faith*.

"If any man draw back, my soul shall have no pleasure in him." *Draw back* means "to take in sail."

But we are not of them who draw back unto perdition; but of them that believe to the saving of the soul [Heb. 10:39].

The writer to the Hebrews did not consider that they had drawn back, but he is speaking of the *danger* of doing so, and he is giving them this warning. Since *draw back* means "to take in sail," the believer is like a sailor who should let out all the sail. That is what the writer has been telling these folk—"Let us go on!" His thought is that a believer could reef his sails—become stranded because of discouragement, because of persecution, because of hardship, because of depression. But since we have a living Savior, let's go on. Let's open up all the sails. Let's move out for God.

You remember the story of the French Huguenots. They were persecuted, and they were betrayed. When France destroyed them, it destroyed the best of French manhood and womanhood. The French Huguenots went into battle, knowing they were facing certain death, and their motto was: "If God be for us, who can be against us?" The nation of France has never since been the nation it was before it destroyed these people.

We believers today need a motto like the Huguenots. There is a lot of boo-hooing today among Christians. There is a lot of complaining and criticizing. There are a bunch of crybabies and babies that need to be burped.

Oh, my Christian friend, the whole tenor of this marvelous epistle is "Let us go on." So let us go on for God!

CHAPTER 11

THEME: Faith

CHRIST BRINGS BETTER BENEFITS AND DUTIES

Chapters 11—13 constitute the second major division of the Epistle to the Hebrews. Up to this point the epistle has largely dealt with that which is doctrinal, but we are now coming to that which is very practical. We begin with the chapter that is often called "the faith chapter," and that is very interesting because the average person does not think that faith is a very practical sort of thing—we will find that it is.

Chapter 11 is also called by many "the catalog of the heroes of faith." I want to look at this chapter from the viewpoint of faith—what faith has done in the lives of men and women in all ages, under all circumstances, from the very gate of the Garden of Eden down to the present moment. This chapter illustrates this for you and me, and these people are witnesses who encourage us to live by faith.

It is so easy to make the Christian life a series of rules. One of the reasons that so many people like to get under the Sermon on the Mount or the Ten Commandments is because men love rules and regulations. It seems so simple and easy to obey rules. Whenever I drive to a new location, I always ask the individual to tell me how to get there. They generally write it out for me: "Turn left here, go so many blocks, and then turn right." I like it that way because it is easy to follow. Life is like that for a great many folk—they want to follow a neat set of rules. But in this chapter we are going to find people who went an altogether different route. They walked by faith, and that is the way God wants us to walk today.

We will also see in this chapter that unbelief is the worst sin anyone can commit. God has a remedy for every sin but the *state* of unbelief. This does not mean that there is an unpardonable sin. There is no *act* which you could commit today that God would not forgive tomorrow.

But if you continue in a state of unbelief, God has no remedy for that at all.

DEFINITION OF FAITH

The first statement in this chapter is a scriptural definition of faith:

> **Now faith is the substance of things hoped for, the evidence of things not seen [Heb. 11:1].**

God has two ways in which men can come to Him today. The first is that you can come to Him by works. Yes, if you can present perfection in your works, God will accept you—but so far nobody has been able to make it. Adam didn't, and no one since has ever been able to do it. Abraham didn't, and David didn't, and Daniel didn't. None of them made it by being perfect. Therefore, this is not a satisfactory way to come to God, but many people are hobbling along that futile route.

The only other way to come to God is to come by faith. Many folk don't find faith a very satisfactory way either and feel like the little girl who was asked to define faith. She said, "Well, faith is believing what you know ain't so." That is what faith means to many. They think it is a leap in the dark, an uncertainty, or some sort of a gamble. If that is what it means to you, then you do not have faith, because "faith is the substance of things hoped for, the evidence of things not seen," which means that faith rests on a foundation.

To other folk faith is a great mystery. It is a sort of sixth sense, some intuition into the spiritual realm, or an open sesame to a new world. Faith to some of these people is like belonging to a secret order into which you are initiated, and there are some mystical works which God will accept in lieu of good works if you just believe hard enough. My friend, the demons do a pretty good job of believing, and they are not saved. There are a lot of cults and "isms" today which are demonic and are run by demons. Faith for these people is like a fetish or some good luck charm which you hang around your neck or carry with you. But that is not faith.

Charles Haddon Spurgeon said: "It is not thy hold on Christ that saves thee; it is Christ. It is not thy joy in Christ that saves thee; it is Christ. It is not even thy faith in Christ that saves thee, though that be the instrument. It is Christ's blood and merit." That is what saves you, my friend. Faith just lays hold of it—that is all. Faith, therefore, is not something mysterious at all—it is that which looks to the Lord Jesus Christ.

Faith is not something which is added to good works. Some folk in our churches today treat faith like it is the dressing which is added to the salad of good works. You have a salad and you put French dressing on it, or bleu cheese dressing, or Italian dressing. Many people just add their faith as a dressing on top of their good works. My friend, that is not faith at all.

Let's look at the scriptural definition of faith that is given to us here: "Faith is the substance of things hoped for, the evidence of things not seen." I like very much what Dr. J. Oswald Sanders (of the China Inland Mission which is now called the Overseas Missionary Fellowship) said: "Faith enables the believing soul to treat the future as present and the invisible as seen." That is good.

"Faith is the *substance* of things hoped for." The Greek word for "substance" is *hupostasis*. It is a scientific term, the opposite of hypothesis or theory. It is that which rests upon facts. In chemistry it would be the chemical which settles at the bottom of the test tube after you have made an experiment.

In my college chemistry class the teacher would give each one of us students a test tube and ask us to find out what was in it. I would take some of whatever was in the tube and add another chemical or two to it and heat it on the Bunsen burner to discover what was in the tube. One day I nearly blew up the laboratory with my experiment because something had been put in the test tube which should not have been put there. Five years later the janitor who swept out the laboratory told me he was still sweeping up little pieces of the big glass Florentine receiver which I had used in my experiment! Fortunately, the glass flew only onto my vest and not into my eyes. I experimented with one test tube for two weeks before I went to the professor to tell him what I thought was in it. I said it was a certain kind of powder and he told me I was right. I had a substance in the bottom of the test tube, and the professor, because he knew his chemistry, was sure of what it was (I'll be honest with you, I wasn't too sure!). But that substance in the bottom of the test tube was what I was looking for. That is the reality. And that is what faith is—faith is a substance.

Dr. A. T. Robertson translates *substance* as "title deed." What is the title deed? What is the substance? It is the Word of God, my friend. If your faith does not rest upon the Word of God, it is not biblical faith at all. It has to rest upon what God says. Actually, it means *to believe God*.

The question is whether you believe God or not. Don't come up with the "I've got intellectual problems" excuse, because that won't work. The thing that keeps men from the Word of God is *sin*. It is sin in your life that keeps you from coming to God. It is the heart that needs to believe—it is "the heart that believeth unto righteousness." When you are ready to give up your sin, the Holy Spirit will make real to you the Word of God.

A very fine man who heads up a wonderful Christian organization in this country sent me (and other ministers) a book he had written and requested my evaluation of it. It is a very fine book, but it is in the realm of apologetics, proving that the Bible is the Word of God. It is one of the best books on the subject I've seen, and I told him so. But I also told him very candidly that I have come to the place in my ministry where a book like that is of no value to me. I already believe the Bible to be the Word of God. I've already been through all those little experiments. I have proven what it is. I *know* the Bible is the Word of God. I've put it *all* in the test tube. I've made the experiment. "Faith is the *substance* of things hoped for." I know it is the Word of God. The Spirit of God has made it real to me.

Paul wrote to the Colossian believers, "For this cause we also, since the day we heard it, do not cease to pray for you, and to desire that ye might be filled with the knowledge of his will in all wisdom and spiritual understanding" (Col. 1:9). To know the will of God is to know the Word of God. He prayed that they might know the Word of God. The Greek word for "knowledge" which Paul used is *epignōsis*. There were Gnostics in that day who professed to have super knowledge. Paul told the Colossians that he wanted them to have super knowledge which was genuine by *knowing* that the Bible is the Word of God, and he believed that the Holy Spirit would make it real to them.

Don't misunderstand me: I did go through a period in college when I almost gave up the ministry. I had an unbelieving professor who was an ordained Presbyterian preacher. I admired the man because he was an intellectual, but he was taking the rug out from under me and taking it out fast. The things he was teaching were about to rob me of my faith, and I had to go to God in prayer. Then I met a man who had two degrees for every degree the first professor had, and this man put me back on the track. He showed me that there were answers for the questions the other man had raised. So I have the answers for myself. I've got a substance in my test tube, and I don't need to make any more experiments today. I *know* the Bible is the Word of God.

Therefore faith rests upon the Word of God. Our dogmatism comes from the Book. That is the reason the writer to the Hebrews said in Hebrews 10:39, "But we are not of them who draw back unto perdition; but of them that believe to the saving of the soul." There are only two ways to go. Either you are going backwards, or you are going to go forwards. Anything that is alive cannot stand still. Out yonder in the forest there is regression and deterioration taking place, but there is also growth and development. Nothing alive out there is standing still—it *cannot.*

"The *evidence* of things not seen." We have seen that faith is the substance of things hoped for—that is scientific. The second word used here is "evidence." In the Greek the word is *elegchos.* It is a legal term meaning "evidence that is accepted for conviction." When I was studying classical Greek in college, I observed that this word is used about twenty-three times in Plato's account of the trial of Socrates. Evidence is something you take into court to prove your case. It is that which the entire business world rests upon. Business is transacted by faith. I have a credit card, and when I drive into the gasoline station I hand it to the attendant. When he takes the card, he believes the oil company will pay him; he believes that I am the owner of the card and that I am the one who will pay for the gasoline in the long run. I say that man has a lot of faith. The oil company also believes that I'm going to pay. (Actually, they *know* I am going to pay, because they will take away my card if I don't!) But the whole transaction takes place by faith. Any man who accepts a check written to him by another is moving by faith. This is *elegchos*, evidence which is accepted in a court of law.

Faith is not a leap in the dark. Faith is not a hope-so. Faith is *substance* and *evidence*—substance for a scientific mind, and evidence for a legal mind. If you really want to believe, you can believe. You can believe a whole lot of foolish things, but God doesn't want you to do that. He wants your faith to rest upon the Word of God.

For by it the elders obtained a good report [Heb. 11:2].

Who are "the elders"? The elders could be one of three different groups. It could be just a group of old people, or it could refer to the office of elder in the New Testament church. Remember that Paul told young Titus that he was to appoint elders in the churches. Or, finally, "elders" could refer to Old Testament saints. These saints were referred to in Hebrews 1:1, "God, who at sundry times and in divers manners spake in time past unto *the fathers*. . . ." The fathers are the elders. This verse could be rendered, "By such faith as this the fathers received witness." These Old Testament worthies believed God, and for them it was not a leap in the dark and it was not a hope-so. Their faith rested upon evidence. Noah built an ark, and he did it by faith. What kind of faith? Was it just some dream he had? No. God gave him an abundance of evidence because Noah *walked* with God for many years.

The problem with many of us today is that when a crisis comes to us and we ought to be able to rest in God and lay hold of Him, we are not able to do so. When we haven't been doing it all along, it is such a new experience for us that it is very difficult to do. However, if you learn to trust God when the sun is shining, it is easier to trust Him on the day when there are dark and lowering clouds in the sky and you are in one of life's storms.

"The elders obtained a good report." Because they were wonderful people? No, because they *believed* God. I think Abraham was a wonderful man. He probably had more going for him than the best Christian today. Even the world would have counted him an outstanding individual. But we are told that it was by faith that Abraham believed God. "Abraham believed God and it was counted to him for righteousness" (see Gen. 15:6). God put righteousness to his account, not because of his good works, but because he *believed God*. "The elders obtained a good report," and they did it by faith.

God wants us today not only to be saved by faith, but also to *walk* by faith. Christ died down here to save us—we look back in faith to Him. Now we walk daily by faith—we look up to Him, the living Christ. That gets right down where the rubber meets the road. That's for right now. Are you going shopping today? Are you going to work? Are you going to school or to some social engagement? Well, then go by faith in the Lord Jesus Christ. We walk by faith, not by sight. That is how God wants us to live this life.

> **Through faith we understand that the worlds were framed by the word of God, so that things which are seen were not made of things which do appear [Heb. 11:3].**

There are two explanations for the origin of this universe. One is speculation, and the other is revelation. By faith we accept revelation, and, my friend, by faith you will accept speculation. Speculation has many theories, and many of them have been abandoned. Right now the theory is evolution, but even evolution, I am told, is going out of style today. It is the best the unbeliever can hold on to, but it is mere speculation, and they have to have a whole lot of faith to go along with it!

"Through faith we understand that the worlds were framed by the word of God." Actually, this could read, "the ages were set up by the Word of God." The Word of God, we have already been told, is quick and powerful and sharper than any two-edged sword. The Word of God is more powerful than an atom or hydrogen bomb. Someone has said that atom bombs come in three sizes: "big," "bigger," and "where is everybody?" Well, the Word of God is even more potent than that, because the Word of God has the power to transform lives. And when you and I come to the Word of God, we either accept or reject God's statement concerning the origin of the universe: "In the beginning God created the heaven and the earth" (Gen. 1:1). That is revelation. Either you believe God, or you go by speculation. Don't tell me that evolution is scientific. It is not. If it were, then all the scientists would be in agreement—and they certainly are *not* in agreement. Today many outstanding scientists are beginning to let go of their worship of evolution. They see so many fallacies in it that they are moving away from it. You either believe God (that's revelation), or you believe speculation. Faith must be anchored in something.

I heard this whimsical story about a guide in a museum who was taking a group of people through the museum and they came to a reconstructed dinosaur. You know how they find one bone and make up the rest of it so that they have a great big dinosaur! Well, the guide said, "This dinosaur is two million and six years old!"

Of course, the crowd looked at him in amazement, and one extrovert said, "What do you mean two million and six years old? Where did you get the *six*?"

"Well," the guide said, "when I came to work here six years ago, it was two million years old. Now it is two million and six years old!" My friend, that shows how utterly ridiculous all this dating—which goes back millions of years—can really become.

Faith means that you have a solid basis for the origin of the universe. I won't have to change my theory as scientific knowledge grows; it has been in operation a long time: "God created the heaven and the earth."

We come now to consider the faith of individuals. I want to give you a quotation from *The Triumphs of Faith* by Dr. G. Campbell Morgan which is fitting at this point. He said, "Life is to be mastered by faith, and not by doubt; it is to be forevermore illuminated by hope, and not darkened by despair; and in its activity love is to be practised in fellowship." We are going to see this illustrated as we consider the lives of these people. Faith is not some jewel like a diamond which you put in a case and look at. That is the reason I do not want to call this chapter a catalog of the heroes of faith. These are men and women who got right down to the nitty-gritty of life—faith was operative in their lives.

Faith is not something which you put on display in a showcase. Faith rests upon the Word of God.

We are given here the experience of three individuals who lived before the Flood—antediluvians we call them (one of them even lived through the Flood and after it). Abel is the first, and in him you have the *way* of faith. Then in Enoch we have the *walk* of faith. And in Noah we have the *witness* of faith. These men lived before the Flood, and faith was in operation at that time. These men walked by faith, lived by faith, and were saved by faith.

THE FAITH OF ABEL

Now with Abel God put down the principle once and for all that men must approach Him on only one basis: by faith, and that salvation will be by faith in Christ. Not only did Abraham see Christ's day and rejoice, but so did Abel.

> **By faith Abel offered unto God a more excellent sacrifice than Cain, by which he obtained witness that he was righteous, God testifying of his gifts: and by it he being dead yet speaketh [Heb. 11:4].**

I want to go back to the Book of Genesis and the story of these two boys, Cain and Abel. I want us to see just what it was that Abel had and Cain didn't have. What was the difference between these two boys?

In Genesis 4:1 we read, "And Adam knew Eve his wife; and she conceived, and bare Cain, and said, I have gotten a man from the LORD." What she really said was, "I have gotten *the* man from the Lord." What man is she talking about? Well, God had made it clear to Eve that there would be coming one in her line, "the seed of the woman." Speaking to Satan, God said, "And I will put enmity between thee and the woman, and between thy seed and her seed; it shall bruise thy head, and thou shalt bruise his heel" (Gen. 3:15). But, you see, Adam and Eve did not know that the struggle with sin was going to last so long. They thought their first son would be the man who was coming to defeat Satan, but Cain was not the Savior; he was a murderer.

We read further in Genesis 4:2, "And she again bare his brother Abel. And Abel was a keeper of the sheep, but Cain was a tiller of the ground." We ought to stop here and make a comparison between the boys, because they were actually antipodes apart, although they were brothers, the sons of Adam and Eve. The late Dr. Henry Rimmer thought they were twins. I don't think they were twins, but I do think they were more alike than twins today could possibly be. For instance, in a family today you can have two boys, and the first boy might be a fine, upstanding boy. He goes through school, makes straight A's, goes to college, and then becomes a professional man, perhaps a doctor. But the other boy doesn't do well in school at all, and he drops out. He begins to drink and to smoke marijuana and get into trouble. Now what is the explanation? The psychologist will come along and say that according to the Mendelian theory the upstanding young man has taken after an ancestor on the mother's side of the family, but the other boy takes after an ancestor on the father's side. That is the explanation that is often given, but you cannot use that method with Cain and Abel. Who were the ancestors of Cain and Abel? They didn't even have grandparents. You cannot use the explanation of heredity for the difference in these two boys. I think they were as alike as two peas in a pod—they looked alike and acted alike in many ways, but they were different.

Neither can you use the explanation of environment as making the difference between Cain and Abel. A great many people today think that environment is what makes the real difference between men. They say that if we could just make the environment all right, every person would be all right. If we could just get rid of the slums and put people into nice homes, then the people would be nice also. But it doesn't always work that way. These two boys had the same environment. I cannot think of a home that was as much the same for two boys as was the home of Cain and Abel.

Genesis 4:3 goes on to say, "And in process of time it came to pass, that Cain brought of the fruit of the ground an offering unto the LORD." "In the process of time" means at the end of days. I think it was the

Sabbath day, for these boys belonged to the first creation, the old creation. They came at a specified time.

"That Cain brought"—the word *brought* has in it the thought that it was brought to an appointed place.

"And Abel, he also brought of the firstlings of his flock and of the fat thereof. And the LORD had respect unto Abel and to his offering: But unto Cain and to his offering he had not respect. And Cain was very wroth, and his countenance fell" (Gen. 4:4–5). Now what was the difference between the two offerings? Didn't both of them come in obedience to God? No, they did not. You see, God had revealed to them that they were to bring a sacrifice, a lamb, and that little lamb pointed to Christ. Someone will argue that Genesis does not say that. No, it doesn't say that, but Hebrews 11 does say it: "By faith Abel offered unto God a more excellent sacrifice than Cain." How could he? He came by faith.

What is faith? Let's look at it again: "Faith cometh by hearing, and hearing by the Word of God" (see Rom. 10:17). Abel had a revelation from God. So did Cain. They were both in the same family. But Cain ignored it, and he brought what he wanted to bring, the fruit of the ground—that which *he* had produced. In other words, here is the first man who brought *his works* to God. A lot of people are still coming to God the same way—they come by works. They have done this and that. Cain brought that which he had raised.

But Abel brought a lamb and slew it. If you had been there, you might have asked, "Brother Abel, why are you bringing a lamb?"

He would have said, "God commanded it."

"Do you think the little lamb takes away your sin?"

"Of course not," he would have said. "I just told you that God commanded us to bring it. He said to my mother that there is One coming in her line who is going to be a Savior, and that Person is the One to whom this little lamb points. I am coming by faith, looking to the time when a deliverer and a Savior will come."

There at the very beginning God made clear the way to Himself: "Without shedding of blood, there is no remission of sins." We come to God on the one basis that we are sinners and that the penalty for our sins must be paid. That is the reason a little lamb had to be slain. That little lamb couldn't take away sin, but it foreshadowed the coming of Christ who is "the Lamb of God that taketh away the sin of the world." And it was offered in faith.

Abel's offering pointed to Christ, and he came by faith—that is the way of salvation. God made the way very clear at the beginning, my friend. Today, though a man be a stranger and a wayfaring man and a fool, he need not err therein. God has made it very clear to us: Christ is the way to Himself; God gave Him to die for our sins. Abel, therefore, illustrates to us the *way* of faith—it is the blood-sprinkled way, the way that is Christ.

THE FAITH OF ENOCH

We come now to Enoch, and in him we see the *walk* of faith. If you come to God through Christ, then you are to walk with Him. It is then the walk of the believer that becomes important.

> **By faith Enoch was translated that he should not see death; and was not found, because God had translated him: for before his translation he had this testimony, that he pleased God [Heb. 11:5].**

Genesis 5 is where we find Enoch mentioned for the first time, and it is a very sad chapter. "This is the book of the generations of Adam. In the day that God created man, in the likeness of God made he him" (Gen. 5:1). We are told that Adam lived an hundred and thirty years and begat a son, Seth. Then Adam died, and Seth lived and begat a son. Then Seth died. "In Adam all die"—that is the way that it's been going on for a long, long time. The fifth chapter of Genesis is just like walking through a cemetery and reading what is engraved on the tombstones. It really becomes monotonous, but it is still the rather sad story of mankind even today. It is the same picture as the present hour in which we live. Things haven't changed much—man still dies. Oh, I know we have extended man's life span, but what are a few years when you put them down next to a thousand years, or even eternity?

But in Genesis we read of Enoch: "And Jared lived after he begat

Enoch eight hundred years, and begat sons and daughters: And all the days of Jared were nine hundred sixty and two years: and he died. And Enoch lived sixty and five years, and begat Methuselah: and Enoch walked with God after he begat Methuselah three hundred years, and begat sons and daughters: and all the days of Enoch were three hundred sixty and five years: and Enoch walked with God: and he was not; for God took him" (Gen. 5:19–24). That is the story of Enoch. Genesis 5 gives us a certain genealogy; it follows a very definite line. We are told that all these begat sons and daughters, but we are not told anything about them. Just one particular son is lifted out—Enoch, the son of Jared.

We are told that Enoch lived sixty-five years and begat a son by the name of Methuselah. Enoch had other children, but apparently his firstborn was Methuselah. "And Enoch walked with God after he begat Methuselah." I do not know what he did before he begat Methuselah, but I'm sure he did not walk with God. It might have been a careless life. It could have been a life that was lived in indifference, or perhaps in open sin. The record does not say. It simply says that he walked with God *after* he begat Methuselah. One day he went into the nursery and looked down into the crib at that little fellow who was kicking and gooing—his name was Methuselah. We always think of Methuselah as being an old man who had such a long beard that it got in his way and he walked on it. But at this time he was just a little baby, and when this man Enoch looked down at that little baby, he recognized his responsibility, and it changed his life. He started to walk with God.

My friend, if the presence of a baby in the home won't change your life-style, nothing else will. Even the preacher won't be able to say much that will affect you, but these little ones have a way of speaking for God, even though they don't say a word. They come out of the everywhere into the here, and they seem so fresh, and somehow or other they bring a message from God. Certainly Methuselah did for this man Enoch, and it changed his life-style.

The record tells us that after Methuselah, Enoch had other children, but it does not tell us that he died. Notice: "And Enoch walked with God: and he was not; for God took him." In Enoch we see the *walk* of faith. The writer to the Hebrews says, "By faith Enoch was translated that he should not see death . . . for before his translation he had this testimony, that he pleased God." His walk pleased God because he walked by faith, not by rules and regulations. He believed in God, and he walked in a manner that pleased Him. Then God took him. He didn't die—he was translated. This is the first rapture of a man recorded in the Bible. He was removed from this earth's scene and was taken away.

We have quite a picture here, by the way, which I think has a spiritual message for us. There are those who believe the church will go through the Great Tribulation Period, and they have used Noah as an example. But Noah represents, not the church, but those in the world who are going to be saved during the Great Tribulation. God is going to keep them. Who are they? They are the 144,000 of Israel and also a great company of Gentiles. They are not part of the body of believers that we designate as the church. We are told in the Book of Revelation that before the winds of the Great Tribulation begin to blow across the earth and the four horsemen of the apocalypse begin to ride, 144,000 out of the nation Israel will be sealed and also a great company of Gentiles. *These* are represented by Noah. My friend, God *can* keep you in the Great Tribulation, but it is not a question of whether or not God can keep you, the question is what God *says*, and He says He is going to *remove* the believers. He told the church in Philadelphia, "Because thou hast kept the word of my patience, I also will keep thee from the hour of temptation, which shall come upon all the world, to try them that dwell upon the earth" (Rev. 3:10). What hour is going to try the earth? The only one mentioned in Scripture is the Great Tribulation Period. This great company of both Jews and Gentiles is to be kept— and Noah represents them. Enoch is the man who represents the church. Enoch didn't go through the Flood. He had been translated. He was not in the ark. God could have put him in the ark, but He didn't. He could have kept Enoch in safety during the Flood, but instead He removed him, and that is what He is going to do with the church—Enoch represents the church.

"By faith Enoch was translated." *Translated* is a good translation, because it means to take something out of one language and put it into another. I have enjoyed listening to the tapes of our radio Bible study broadcasts in Spanish although I can't understand a word that is being said. The man who is giving my message in Spanish is reading it, but you would never know it. He's doing an excellent job. The manager of the station in South America says they have everything in that broadcast except my Texas accent! Well, I like the way the man does it, and it is a translation. It was taken out of the English language and put into the Spanish language for South America.

Enoch was translated out of one sphere of life and translated into another. The best way I know to describe it is the way it was told by a little girl who came home from Sunday school, and her mother asked, "What did your teacher tell you about today?"

The little girl said, "She told us all about this man Enoch." You can see that this was a good Bible teaching Sunday school.

And the mother said, "Well, what about Enoch?"

So the little girl told her mama this story: "Enoch lived a long time ago, and God would come by every afternoon and say to him, 'Enoch, would you like to take a walk with Me?' Enoch would say, 'Yes, I'd like to take a walk with You, God.' And so every day God would come by Enoch's house, and Enoch would go walking with God. One day God came by and said, 'Enoch, let's take a long walk today. I want to talk to you.' So they started out. Enoch got his coat—even took his lunch, and they started walking. They walked and they walked and they walked, and finally it got late. Enoch said, 'My, it's getting late, and I am a long way from home. Maybe we'd better start back.' But God said, 'Enoch, you are closer to My home than you are to your home, so you come on and go home with Me.' And so Enoch went home with God." I don't know how to tell the story any better than that. And that is what will happen one day with the church. The church, that is, the body of true believers, walking with God like Enoch was, will one day go home with Him. The Lord Jesus is coming: "For the Lord himself shall descend from heaven with a shout, with the voice of the archangel, and with the trump of God: and the dead in Christ shall rise first: Then we which are alive and remain shall be caught up together with them in the clouds, to meet the Lord in the air: and so shall we ever be with the Lord" (1 Thess. 4:16–17).

> **But without faith it is impossible to please him; for he
> that cometh to God must believe that he is, and that he is
> a rewarder of them that diligently seek him [Heb. 11:6].**

"But without faith it is impossible to please him." Enoch pleased God. How did he do it? By faith. My friend, unless you are willing to come God's way and believe Him, you cannot possibly please God.

"For he that cometh to God must believe that he is, and that he is a rewarder of them that diligently seek him." In this Hebrew epistle there is a great deal said about rewards, and the reason is that the emphasis is on the Christian life. In light of the fact that we have a living Savior up there who is for us, there is a reward for living the Christian life. But salvation is *not* a reward—it is a free gift. You work for your reward, but not for salvation. Salvation comes by faith, and the walk of the Christian is also by faith. Enoch walked with God by faith.

THE FAITH OF NOAH

> **By faith Noah, being warned of God of things not seen
> as yet, moved with fear, prepared an ark to the saving of
> his house; by the which he condemned the world, and
> became heir of the righteousness which is by faith [Heb.
> 11:7].**

Abel showed the way of faith; Enoch illustrated the walk of faith; and now Noah is the *witness* of faith.

"By faith Noah . . . to the saving of his house." Many of us are accustomed to saying that Noah preached 120 years and never made a convert. Actually, that is not quite accurate. It is true that he didn't win any of the Babylonians living there in Babel, but he surely won his family. He led every member of his family to the Lord, and that was really something.

Again, we need to go back to Genesis and look closely at this man Noah. We are told in Genesis 6:5, "And God saw that the wickedness of man was great in the earth, and that every imagination of the thoughts of his heart was only evil continually." That is a sad commentary on mankind. Man surely got away from God in a hurry after he left the Garden of Eden. However, we are told that there was one godly man left: "These are the generations of Noah: Noah was a just man and perfect in his generations, and Noah walked with God" (Gen. 6:9). Does this mean he was only a nice man who paid his debts and did many helpful things for people? No, he did more than that: "Noah walked with God." How did he walk with God? The writer to the Hebrews tells us: "*By faith* Noah, being warned of God of things not seen as yet, moved with fear, prepared an ark to the saving of his house."

This man Noah believed God when God told him He was going to destroy the earth by a flood. There are some people who suggest that up to this point it had never even rained on the earth—and that is probably true. But way up on dry ground, probably near Mount Ararat, away from even the Euphrates River, this man Noah began to build a boat because God said there was going to be a flood.

God gave Noah the instructions for the boat. It wasn't that clumsy-looking thing that you see pictured in Sunday school papers. When I was a little boy, my thought was, *I'd sure hate to be in that boat!* Probably it was very modern-looking equipment, and the size and construction of it would conform to modern ship building. We are told that the length of it was 300 cubits, the breadth of it was 50 cubits, and the height of it was 30 cubits. And it didn't have just one little window in the side. God said to Noah, "A window shalt thou make to the ark, and in a cubit shalt thou finish it above; and the door of the ark shalt thou set in the side thereof; with lower, second, and third stories shalt thou make it" (Gen. 6:16). The window went all the way around the top, and the roof came down over it. The ark was 300 cubits, or about 450 feet, long, and it had three decks. The men in that day were good builders and they were familiar with this type of construction. Therefore Noah began to do what I'm sure the population in his day considered to be a very foolish thing. I'm of the opinion that the sightseeing buses ran a tour out to where he was building the boat—and I'm sure it was a popular tour.

I have often wondered what it was that brought Noah's three sons, Ham, Shem, and Japheth, back home. These boys, I'm sure, had moved away and started their own businesses. Perhaps Ham was a contractor, a successful builder himself, down in Babel. Maybe one day he was meeting with a contractors' convention where he heard a man telling about a trip he'd made to the north country. There he had heard of a man who was building a boat on dry ground. He felt it was really ridiculous, and everybody agreed, including Ham. But then Ham, knowing his dad lived up there and having heard some things about his dad, asked the man if he had seen the boat builder. The man said he had seen the builder and the builder's name was Noah. Ham probably turned white when he heard that. He stood up and said, "Listen, that's my father who is building that boat. I agree with you—it sounds foolish. I laughed as you laughed, but you don't know my dad. My dad walks in the fear of the living God. I've gotten away from that, but if my dad says a flood is coming, it's because God has caused him to give out a message of warning. You can just put it down that God has spoken to him and a flood is coming. I was brought up in that home, and I know that I might cut corners but my dad wouldn't. My dad never told a lie. My dad lived for God. If you don't mind, I'm going to get my hammer and saw, and I'm going up there to help him build that boat!" I think Shem and Japheth had similar experiences and went back home to help their dad. Why? Because this man Noah had a witness for God.

My friend, I say this very candidly, the most important thing you can do is to witness to your own family—not by everlastingly giving them the Gospel, but by living it before them and letting them see that you have a reality in your life. This reminds me of an encounter that Gypsy Smith had when he was holding meetings in Dallas, Texas. A lady came up and told him that God had called her to preach. He felt the same way about women preachers as I do, and so he asked her if she was married. She was. He said, "How many children do you have?" She had five children. "Isn't that wonderful," Gypsy told her, "God has called you to preach, and He's already given you a congregation!" May I say to you, whether you are a preacher or not, if you are a child of God and you have a family, that is your congregation. God gave you that congregation. Noah won his family. No one outside his family believed, but his family believed because they knew his witness. Noah "prepared an ark to the saving of his house." What a wonderful thing that he was able to do that!

THE FAITH OF ABRAHAM AND SARAH

We come now to Abraham, the man who is known as the man of faith. That is the way he is identified in the Word of God. Abraham is the supreme illustration of faith in the Epistle to the Romans and also in the Epistle to the Galatians. The writers of the Gospels refer to him, and even the Lord Jesus said, "Your father Abraham rejoiced to see my day: and he saw it, and was glad" (John 8:56). In Abraham we will see the *worship* of faith.

> **By faith Abraham, when he was called to go out into a place which he should after receive for an inheritance, obeyed; and he went out, not knowing whither he went [Heb. 11:8].**

We have seen in this epistle that the worship of God leads to obedience to God. It leads to work for God. It leads to doing the thing God wants you to do. We do not need to spend time browbeating people, telling them they should get busy for God—that is not the proper motivation. But if they can truly worship God and catch something of the glory of the person of Christ, then you can depend on them to work for God and to obey Him. The most important word in this verse and in this entire section is *obeyed*, and worship leads to obedience.

In Genesis 12 where the story of Abraham begins, we read that he came out of Ur of the Chaldees and went to Haran. He delayed in Haran and lost a great deal of time, but finally he went to the land of Canaan. When he appeared in the land, God appeared to him. "And the LORD appeared unto Abram, and said, Unto thy seed will I give this land: and there builded he an altar unto the LORD, who appeared unto him" (Gen. 12:7). Everywhere this man went he built an altar. When he came into the land of Shechem he built an altar. When he went down to the plains of Moreh he built an altar unto the Lord. Everywhere Abra-

ham went he built an altar to God. I have been impressed on my trips
to the Holy Land with the number of buildings that Herod put up. He
not only built the temple, which was never really completed, but he
also built palaces and forts and cities all over that land. But there was
no actual worship of God on his part. All Abraham did was put up an
altar, but he worshipped God, and that led to obedience of God. He
worshipped God by faith; then he obeyed God by faith.

> **By faith he sojourned in the land of promise, as in a
> strange country, dwelling in tabernacles with Isaac and
> Jacob, the heirs with him of the same promise:**

> **For he looked for a city which hath foundations, whose
> builder and maker is God.**

> **Through faith also Sara herself received strength to
> conceive seed, and was delivered of a child when she
> was past age, because she judged him faithful who had
> promised [Heb. 11:9–11].**

When God told Sarah at ninety years of age that she was to have a
child, she laughed because it was ridiculous—it seemed utterly pre-
posterous. She couldn't accept it, but God gave her the strength and
power to believe Him. Many of us need such strength. Do you remember the man who brought the demon-possessed boy to the Lord Jesus?
The Lord Jesus told the man that He could help him if he would believe. The man said, "I believe. Help thou mine unbelief." The man
recognized that he had a weak faith, but the Lord Jesus must have
given him the faith because He healed the boy (see Mark 9:17–27).
Sarah had a little boy named Isaac. Why? She "received strength to
conceive seed, and was delivered of a child when she was past age,
because she judged him faithful who had promised." Sarah represents
the *power* (or strength) of faith.

> **Therefore sprang there even of one, and him as good as
> dead, so many as the stars of the sky in multitude, and
> as the sand which is by the sea shore innumerable [Heb.
> 11:12].**

This is what happened, and it all took place by faith. But notice that Abraham and Sarah never saw the fulfillment of God's promise to them:

> **These all died in faith, not having received the promises, but having seen them afar off, and were persuaded of them, and embraced them, and confessed that they were strangers and pilgrims on the earth [Heb. 11:13].**

Walking by faith will cause all of us to recognize that as children of God we are just pilgrims and strangers down here on this earth.

> **For they that say such things declare plainly that they seek a country [Heb. 11:14].**

Faith looks out yonder to the future. And the child of God today is looking to the future.

I am not in the employ of the local chamber of commerce, but I very frankly love Southern California. I have lived here longer than I've lived any place in my life—since 1940—and I love it, in spite of the smog and the traffic and all these people who followed us out here. I wish we could have put a wall around California (after *we* got here, of course!), and then we could have had this wonderful place to ourselves. All of us who have come out here certainly haven't helped the place, but I still prefer it to any other. I have a "ranch" out here in California. It's not what you call a big ranch—it's about 72 feet wide and about 128 feet deep. But I have my house right in the middle of it, and I have it well stocked. I have orange trees, avocado trees, tangerine trees, nectarine trees, apricots, plums, and lemons. You see, I'm really a rancher. The other day I just looked up and thanked the Lord that He gave me that place. It is the first place I have ever owned and paid for, but *He* gave it to me, and I thank Him for it. However, I told Him, "Don't let me get in love with this place, or I won't want to leave it to go to a better place." We are strangers and pilgrims down here, because we are walking by faith, looking to a better place. "For they that say such things declare plainly that they seek a country."

> **And truly, if they had been mindful of that country from whence they came out, they might have had opportunity to have returned.**
>
> **But now they desire a better country, that is, an heavenly: wherefore God is not ashamed to be called their God: for he hath prepared for them a city [Heb. 11:15–16].**

Anyone can turn around and go back to the world if he is satisfied with the things of the world. However, a child of God, by faith, is going ever onward.

> **By faith Abraham, when he was tried, offered up Isaac; and he that had received the promises offered up his only begotten son [Heb. 11:17].**

Now we come to the end of Abraham's life, and the supreme sacrifice he made in offering up Isaac, the boy that God had given to him.

> **Of whom it was said, That in Isaac shall thy seed be called [Heb. 11:18].**

Abraham had other children, but Isaac is the one called "his only begotten." (The word *son* in verse 17 is not in the original text.) Isaac was the only begotten because God gave the promise concerning him.

> **Accounting that God was able to raise him up, even from the dead; from whence also he received him in a figure [Heb. 11:19].**

God did not ask Abraham to offer up Isaac until he had come to the end of his life. The reason is that Abraham would not have had the faith to do it. God will never test you "above that ye are able" (see 1 Cor. 10:13). Therefore God never asked Abraham to give up Ishmael, that is, to sacrifice him on an altar. Do you know why? Well, to begin with, Ishmael wasn't the promised son. And the second thing is that Abraham would not have done it, you can be sure. Abraham even begged God not to send Ishmael away but to let him keep the boy and make him the son of promise. You see, Abraham wasn't ready at that time to do such a thing. And certainly at the beginning of Isaac's life when he was just a baby, Abraham never would have offered him. When Isaac was about thirty-three years of age, Abraham was ready to obey God and trust Him. Therefore, we have here the testing of faith.

I want to look at Abraham a little bit differently from the way we ordinarily see him. We usually think in terms of the great promises which God made to him concerning the land to be given to him and the multitudes which would come from him. But what was it that Abraham actually *received* during his lifetime? What was it that he actually saw? He did not see the fulfillment of those great promises, but what God did give to him was a home. When he was a young man living in Ur of the Chaldees, he one day said to a beautiful young girl, "I love you. I want to marry you." And so Abraham and Sarah got married.

Then one day Abraham came home—it was a home of idolatry—and he said to Sarah, "The living God has called me. He wants me to leave this place."

I can just hear Sarah say, "But you have a good business. All your relatives live here. Your friends live here. And, by the way, *where* are you going?"

Abraham would have to say, "I don't know."

"What do you mean that God called you and you don't know where?"

He said, "God will lead me, and I'm going out."

And Sarah said, "I'll go with you." And so this young couple went out. They didn't have too much faith. They took papa with them and some of the relatives, and they came to Haran. They hung around Haran until Papa Terah died and they buried him.

Then Abraham moved into the land and God appeared to him. God said to him, "Abraham, I am going to do all these things I promised, but I am also going to give you a son." Now that is what is going to make the home—Abraham and Sarah are going to have a son.

Abraham and Sarah had the basis for a godly home in that day. It was the kind of home God wants young people to have today—we call it a Christian home. To establish this godly home God did not give them a course or send them to a preacher for counseling. Frankly, we preachers have done too much counseling, telling young people how they ought to do it. We have become too idealistic, but God was very practical. He said, "Abraham, if you are going to have the kind of home I want you to have, you are going to have to get away from papa and mama." That is what God meant at the very beginning when He said to Adam and Eve, "Therefore shall a man leave his father and his mother, and shall cleave unto his wife: and they shall be one flesh" (Gen. 2:24). Although Adam and Eve didn't even have a mother and father, God set down this great principle at the very beginning.

I never thought that I would be a grandfather who would tell the parents how to raise a child. I didn't do so well myself as a parent, but I have learned that it is the easiest thing in the world to tell them how to do it. Well, they *will* make mistakes, but it is none of my business. We made our mistakes, and they will make theirs. Papa and mama are not to interfere with the home of the children. God set Abraham as far away as possible where relatives were not going to be able to interfere. I think this is primary to building a godly home.

God had Abraham leave his home. It was a godless home he left, a home of idolatry. Joshua made that clear (see Josh. 24:2).

A great many rules and regulations concerning marriage are being given to young couples in our day. I don't want to sound revolutionary, but I do want to say what the Word of God says to do. You can forget the rules and regulations until you are walking by faith. If you are a child of God, you are to walk by faith in that home. The father is to walk by faith and the mother is to walk by faith. And do you want to know something? The home will never be an ideal home. I am weary of hearing folk tell how they went to a counseling session and now they have the most glorious home you have ever heard of. Well, may I say to you, I have been married to my wife for a long time and we disagree on many things. The fact of the matter is, she has a right to be wrong! But we've always been able to come to the place where I could put my arm around her and tell her I love her in spite of the fact that she is wrong.

My young Christian friend, if you think you are going to start an ideal Christian home, I think you are mistaken. You will find that you will be tested just as Abraham was tested when he ran off to Egypt. I am of the opinion that all the way to Egypt, Sarah said, "Abraham, I don't want to go down to Egypt." But they went to Egypt. He almost lost Sarah to someone else down there because he lied and said she was not his wife. That certainly is not an ideal home, is it?

When Abraham returned to the Promised Land from Egypt, we find that he had trouble there with his nephew. Maybe Abraham should have left him in Ur of the Chaldees, but finally Lot moved down to Sodom, leaving Abraham alone up in the hill country. Here again, we see that neither Abraham nor Sarah were what we would call ideal. Abraham doubted God. He didn't believe that God ought to destroy Sodom and Gomorrah. God had to make it clear to him that what He was doing was a righteous and just thing. And He had to make it clear to Sarah that He could give her power to have a son. He gave them that little child to raise in their home.

Abraham and Sarah's home was the kind of home God wants you to have. If you think that following a few little rules is going to avoid all the rough places and hardships in life, you are wrong. You will find out that one day you will argue with your wife. You are going to find out that one day you are going to have a problem with the child God gives you. Your home will not be ideal by any means. How are you going to handle all these problems? By faith, my friend, by faith. When you and I have reached the place where we are willing to put our child upon the altar for God, then you and I have arrived. Abraham and Sarah's home was just about as near to what God wants down here as any of us will be able to attain.

Christian friend, if it is going hard with you and you are having problems, then God is trying to teach you something. Let God be your teacher. Don't run to your pastor or think you can take a course that will solve all your problems. You and I are going to have problems, but if we walk by faith, He will see us through.

Abraham's *worship* of faith led to obedience in his life, so that it could be said of him, ". . . Abraham believed God, and it was counted unto him for righteousness" (Rom. 4:3).

THE FAITH OF ISAAC

**By faith Isaac blessed Jacob and Esau concerning things
to come [Heb. 11:20].**

Notice that very little is said concerning Isaac, especially when it is
in contrast to his father Abraham. What can we say concerning Isaac?
He represents the *willingness* of faith. Isaac was a grown man, probably around thirty-three years of age, when his father Abraham offered
him on the altar. That certainly demonstrates his willingness!

"By faith Isaac blessed Jacob and Esau concerning things to come."
The one thing that is pinpointed in Isaac's life is his faith in blessing
his sons. Now that seems a very strange thing. Isaac was a well digger.
He would dig a well in a certain place, and the enemy would take it
away from him. He would then dig another well, and again it would be
taken away from him. In many ways he was a rather colorless individual, but the thing that characterized him was willingness. He was
willing to bless Jacob and Esau concerning things to come, but there
was nothing in the immediate present that would cause him to bless
them.

THE FAITH OF JACOB

We come now to a very colorful individual—

**By faith Jacob, when he was a-dying, blessed both the
sons of Joseph; and worshipped, leaning upon the top of
his staff [Heb. 11:21].**

This man Jacob lived a life of faith in relationship to his father, and to
his son Joseph, and to his grandsons. But the one thing that was se-
lected out of his life happened when he was dying. You must wait until
the end of this man's life before you can say that he was a man of faith.
At the time of his death he blessed both of the sons of Joseph, his
grandsons, and he worshipped "leaning upon the top of his staff."

There are several things which we can observe from the life of Jacob. He is an illustration of human nature and of the fact that it is by grace that we are saved. If it had not been for the grace of God, Jacob would have been lost. He had no human merit—none whatsoever. I'm not sure but what that is a picture of all of us.

> Nothing in my hand I bring,
> Simply to Thy cross I cling.
> "Rock of Ages"
> —Augustus M. Toplady

Dr. J. Hudson Taylor, founder of the China Inland Mission, had a way of emphasizing the fact that before God we are nothing, and that God is the only one who can take nothing and do something with it. He told the story of a young, self-confident missionary who arrived on the field with his wife. Finally one day the young fellow came to Dr. Taylor and told him that it was difficult for him to think he was nothing. "Young man," Dr. Taylor said, "you *are* nothing, whether you believe it or not. You can just take God's word for it!"

This man Jacob is a picture of our human nature. We hear a great deal today in psychology about prenatal care, natal care, and postnatal care, and how important these are in shaping the life of the individual. The gynecologist and the psychologist give a lot of emphasis to the care of a baby before birth, at birth, and immediately after birth. What can be said of Jacob's life in these respects? The Bible tells us that Jacob and Esau struggled within their mother. Even before birth, Jacob was wrestling and trying to get the upper hand! He struggled even at birth. He came out last, but he came out holding on to the heel of his brother. He was a heel-grabber, and he was that all of his life. Also Jacob was a deceiver and he was a rascal. God, however, *did* transform his life.

First of all, in the life of this man, we find that he was a deceiver in relationship to his father. God had promised Jacob the blessing, but he couldn't wait for it. He took it from his brother Esau by a very deceptive method, which forced him to leave home, and he spent the night in Beth-el. He was very homesick, but no change had taken place in his life. Even when he went down to live with his Uncle Laban he was still relying on his wits. Then God had to stop him when he was finally returning to the land. The Lord wrestled with him that night at the brook Jabbok. That night God crippled him—He had to get Jacob.

Later in the life of Jacob we see that the very sin he committed came home to him in the life of his son Joseph. One day his sons brought that very bloody coat of many colors which belonged to Joseph, and they said to Jacob, "Is this the coat of your son? Do you recognize it?" And Jacob began to weep. In the same way in which he had deceived, he was deceived by his sons into thinking that Joseph had been killed. The sins of the fathers are visited upon the children—this is certainly an example of that.

However, at the end of this man's life, the writer to the Hebrews shows us Jacob's faith in relationship to his grandsons, Ephraim and Manasseh. "By faith Jacob, when he was a-dying. . . ." He is on his deathbed, and this is the first thing in his life you can lift out and say, "By faith Jacob. . . ."

He "blessed both the sons of Joseph; and worshipped." For the first time there will be obedience in his life. It has always interested me that he worshipped "leaning upon the top of his staff." What staff? Remember that he had been crippled, and he had a staff that enabled him to walk. Even when death came, this man did not want to lie down and die. There was no blessing in the *life* of Jacob. It was a life of sin and deception, chicanery and crookedness—and no blessing ever eventuates from sin.

The important thing for you and me to see is that God can take any life and straighten it out. Where there is confusion and deception, if there is faith anchored in the Lord Jesus Christ, we can lay hold of Him. Faith was operative in the life of Jacob, but we have to come to the end of his life to see it.

THE FAITH OF JOSEPH

By faith Joseph, when he died, made mention of the departing of the children of Israel; and gave commandment concerning his bones [Heb. 11:22].

I am confident that the writer to the Hebrews and the Holy Spirit of God could have chosen many incidents from the life of Joseph which would illustrate faith. We could cite the time when this man was down there in Egypt and put into prison. You would think that this was going to be the end for him, and many of us would have cried out in complaint at that time. But that incident was not recorded here. And there are so many other illustrations of faith in the life of this man Joseph. What a contrast he is to his father Jacob! There are no faults or flaws in his life.

There is probably no one in the entire Old Testament who is more closely a type of the Lord Jesus Christ than is Joseph; however, he is never spoken of as a type in Scripture. The analogy between the two is striking. Joseph was the best beloved son as was the Lord Jesus. Joseph had a coat of many colors which set him apart from his brethren and gave him lordship over them; he had a vision and his brethren thought he was a dreamer. The Lord Jesus, too, came with a message, and they thought he was a dreamer. Joseph obeyed his father, and the Lord Jesus said He had come to do the Father's will. Joseph's brethren hated him; it is said of the Lord Jesus, "He came unto his own, and his own received him not" (John 1:11). Joseph was sent by his father to seek his brethren, and the Lord Jesus came to this earth seeking the lost. Joseph found his brothers who were shepherds in a field; shepherds came by night when the Lord Jesus was born. His brethren mocked Joseph, refused him, and plotted to kill him; the same happened to the Lord Jesus. Joseph was sold into slavery, and the Lord was sold for thirty pieces of silver. Joseph's coat was dipped in blood; the soldiers gambled for the vesture of the Lord Jesus Christ, with His blood upon it. Joseph was sold into Egypt where God raised him up to save (in a material way) the world; the Lord Jesus went down into death—after having been tempted by the world, the flesh, and the Devil—to become the Savior of the world—both Jew and Gentile. While on the throne, Joseph gave bread to the people; Christ is the Bread of Life. While in Egypt, Joseph got a gentile bride; the Lord Jesus is calling out of this world a people to His name. Joseph made himself known to his brethren when they came to Egypt; someday the Lord Jesus will make Himself known to His own brethren.

The interesting thing about Joseph is that he had faith in the dream which was given to him, faith while in the pit into which he was placed, faith all the while he was in Egypt, and faith was what buoyed him up through all the adverse circumstances. You would think that at the end of his life he would be satisfied with Egypt—but not this man. He said, "When the day comes that the children of Israel leave this land, be sure and take my bones with you" (see Gen. 50:25). Why didn't they take his body right then and bury it yonder in the land of Ephraim? The reason is quite obvious: this man was a national hero at the time. But there came a day when there rose a pharaoh who knew not Joseph, and when the children of Israel left, they took up his bones and buried them at Shechem in the Samaritan country.

THE FAITH OF MOSES

Now we move down quite a few years to the time when the children of Israel are in slavery in the land of Egypt. Moses represents the *sacrifices* of faith.

> **By faith Moses, when he was born, was hid three months of his parents, because they saw he was a proper child; and they were not afraid of the king's commandment [Heb. 11:23].**

Moses had godly parents who were willing to take a real stand for God. Faith was involved in the very birth of Moses.

> **By faith Moses, when he was come to years, refused to be called the son of Pharaoh's daughter;**
>
> **Choosing rather to suffer affliction with the people of God, than to enjoy the pleasures of sin for a season [Heb. 11:24–25].**

We see faith at work in the life of Moses. He was brought up in the palace and would have been the next pharaoh, but Moses had faith to choose the right.

> **Esteeming the reproach of Christ greater riches than the treasures in Egypt: for he had respect unto the recompence of the reward [Heb. 11:26].**

Someone else other than Abraham saw Christ's day and rejoiced—Moses did.

> **By faith he forsook Egypt, not fearing the wrath of the king: for he endured, as seeing him who is invisible [Heb. 11:27].**

Moses had faith to act—faith will lead to action. Many folk today are saying, "I believe, I believe," but do nothing. May I say, faith reveals itself in action. God saves us without our works, but the faith that saves produces works. Therefore Moses "forsook Egypt, not fearing the wrath of the king: for he endured, as seeing him who is invisible."

> **Through faith he kept the passover, and the sprinkling of blood, lest he that destroyed the firstborn should touch them [Heb. 11:28].**

Moses had faith to obey God. God said to do this, and Moses did it. This is exemplified in the life of this man. He forsook the pleasures of Egypt, went out into the desert, and came back to deliver his people. This is faith to obey God.

> **By faith they passed through the Red sea as by dry land: which the Egyptians assaying to do were drowned [Heb. 11:29].**

Whose faith do we see here? Is this the faith of the children of Israel? No. They had none. When they saw Pharaoh and his chariots coming, they said in effect to Moses, "Let's get back to Egypt as quick as we can! We made a mistake in leaving." It was Moses who had faith. He went down to the water's edge and smote it with that rod; and it was by his faith that the waters opened up and they were able to march over to

the other side. Then they sang the song of Moses. The people are identified with Moses, but this was Moses' faith.

THE FAITH OF JOSHUA

**By faith the walls of Jericho fell down, after they were
compassed about seven days [Heb. 11:30].**

We have in the life of Joshua the *watch* of faith. If you had met Joshua
about the fifth day they were marching around the city of Jericho,
you might have said to him, "It doesn't look like you are getting
very far. Why are you doing such a foolish thing? You are a general
with a whole lot of intelligence, but you are not using your intelligence."

He would have said to you, "You have forgotten that I saw the cap-
tain of the hosts of the Lord, and He told me that headquarters is not in
my tent, but in heaven. I found out that I am not the general. I happen
to be a buck private in the rear ranks, and I am to take my orders from
Him. He said to march around the city, and I am marching around.
You just watch—these walls will come down. I'm following the strat-
egy of Someone who knows."

In Joshua we see the watch of faith. Faith to believe God—General
Joshua had learned that.

THE FAITH OF RAHAB

**By faith the harlot Rahab perished not with them that
believed not, when she had received the spies with
peace [Heb. 11:31].**

I want to call Rahab's story the *wonder* of faith.

Her story is in connection with the story of the walls of Jericho. She
was living inside the city, and I am sure that after seven days those on
the inside were wondering what was going to happen.

"By faith the harlot Rahab perished not with them that believed
not." Many years ago a book was published with the title *Religion in*

Unlikely Places. I do not know if Rahab was included in that book—I never read it—but she certainly should have been. Jericho was the last place in the world you would have looked for faith. Rahab lived in a very wicked, pagan, and heathen city—*and* she practiced the oldest profession there. Those who practice that profession have usually been considered to be sinners—until recently, of course, when the "new morality" came along. This woman was a sinner, and yet we are told here, "by faith the harlot Rahab perished not with them that believed not." I'm sure that the mayor of the city and others who were in high position felt that they were good enough to have been saved, but they were not saved. We are told they perished in the city because of just one reason: they did not believe God.

We will see that God was very generous in the way He dealt with the city of Jericho. I know the critic finds a great deal of fault with God for destroying the people of Jericho. I had a professor in college who could weep crocodile tears because of what happened to the people in the city of Jericho. The thing that always disturbed me about this man was that he showed very little interest in other people—including his students, by the way—but he could really work up a lather when it came to the people of Jericho.

We want to look closely at this woman Rahab, because she expressed her faith in a very definite way. When the people of Israel had crossed over the Red Sea, that word got to Jericho, and the inhabitants of Jericho lost their courage. But they never dreamed that during flood season the great host of Israel could be brought across the Jordan River. There was no bridge on which they could cross, and the river was on a rampage at that time. How in the world could the people get over? The people of Jericho had felt that they had time to plan a defense and didn't have to worry until the flood season was over.

Then Joshua sent spies into the city of Jericho, and they came into contact with the harlot Rahab. I have a notion she made a business proposition to them, but I do not know whether they accepted or not. I do know they made it very clear that they were on a mission, that they needed protection, and that God was going to give the city of Jericho into their hands. They at least gave her that much information. She took them in and hid them on the roof of her house and no doubt risked her own life in doing that. She asked one favor from these men, "When you take this city, I want you to remember me and my family. I want you to save us." And they promised to do that. They told her to put out a scarlet line in the window to identify her house, and that when Joshua took the city he would be very careful to save her and her household.

Rahab's testimony is found in the Book of Joshua: "And she said unto the men, I know that the LORD hath given you the land, and that your terror is fallen upon us, and that all the inhabitants of the land faint because of you. For we have heard how the LORD dried up the water of the Red sea for you, when ye came out of Egypt; and what ye did unto the two kings of the Amorites, that were on the other side Jordan, Sihon and Og, whom ye utterly destroyed. And as soon as we had heard these things, our hearts did melt, neither did there remain any more courage in any man, because of you: for the LORD your God, he is God in heaven above, and in earth beneath" (Josh. 2:9–11).

This is a strange statement that comes from this woman, but it is a tremendous revelation of the fact that God did not arbitrarily destroy the city of Jericho. You see, for *forty* years word had been filtering into Jericho about a people who crossed the Red Sea. In other words, Rahab said, "It was forty years ago when we heard about that. And I for one believed. Others believed the facts, but they did not believe in God. They never trusted the living God." Later on, they heard how God was leading Israel and that He had given them victory on the other side of the Jordan against the Amorites. Jericho should have profited from that information. Finally Israel miraculously crossed the Jordan River and parked right outside the door of Jericho. What had God been doing? He had been giving the city an opportunity to believe in Him, to trust Him, and to turn to Him.

I think it should be obvious to anyone that if God saved this harlot who believed in Him, He would have saved the mayor of Jericho and He would have saved anyone in the city if he had trusted Him as this woman trusted Him. He saw all of them on one basis—He saw them all as sinners. "All have sinned and come short of the glory of God." Rahab probably was a more open sinner than the mayor was. I am of the opinion that the mayor's private life would not have stood inspection, and I am sure that that was true of many others in that city, but they had ample opportunity to trust God. They had forty years to decide whether they would believe God, and they did not.

If that college professor of mine were still alive, there is a question I would love to ask him. God gave them forty years to make up their minds whether they would trust Him or not. Only one woman made up her mind to trust God, and God saved her. It is obvious that since she was saved, anyone else would have been saved if they had trusted God. Now if you think forty years was not quite long enough, do you feel that God probably should have given them forty-*one* or forty-*two* years? My friend, if after forty years they are not going to believe God, they are not ever going to believe God. God is longsuffering. He is patient. He is not willing that any should perish. Even a harlot who will trust Him, God will save. The people of Jericho believed the facts which they heard, but they didn't trust God. If they had, they would have been saved.

Now when this woman evidenced that she believed God by asking the spies to save her when they took the city, she took a step of faith, and in that step of faith she risked her life. Her faith began to move. Faith goes into action—it does not sit on the sidelines. So this woman Rahab "perished not with them that believed not, when she had received the spies with peace." Faith cometh by hearing, and hearing by the Word of God. "We have heard what God has done through you, and we believe it," she said. "I trust Him. I trust Him to the extent that I am willing to risk my life." She evidenced the faith that she had.

We see in this woman Rahab the wonder of faith. We see that in this lost world God doesn't view one group of people as so much better than another group of people. God sees us all as sinners, and when anyone will turn to Him, God will save him. How wonderful He is!

THE FAITH OF "OTHERS"

And what shall I more say? for the time would fail me to tell of Gedeon, and of Barak, and of Samson, and of Jephthae; of David also, and Samuel, and of the prophets [Heb. 11:32].

The writer of this epistle has come to a point in the history of the Old Testament at which he says, "What more can I say now?" He could go in any direction and could list heroes of faith, if you want to call them that. He could demonstrate how faith has worked in the lives of many men and women. So he gives us a list and makes it clear that he is not able to discuss them in detail, but that all should be included in this marvelous chapter.

We see the *war* of faith in the lives of these men he mentions. Not one of them is dealt with in detail, but all have something in common: everyone mentioned here was a ruler. Gideon, Barak, Samson, Jephthah, and Samuel were all judges; David was a king. They were all rulers, and they were all engaged in a war for God. Each one of them won that battle by faith.

I will not be able to go into detail with each of these men, but I would like to take note of this man Gideon. Many people say that all they have in their church is a "little Gideon's band." What they mean is that they have a small number of people. But, my friend, it was not the small number that was significant about Gideon's band—it was the faith these men had. Yet Gideon was a man who actually had very little faith at the time when the Lord called him.

Gideon was a judge at the time the Midianites had taken the land of Israel. The Hebrews couldn't even harvest their crops—the Midianites would take it from them. This young man Gideon was down by the winepress harvesting grain. That is not where he should have been. The grain was usually taken up to the top of the hill, pitched up in the air where the wind could drive the chaff away. In that land the wind blows in the afternoon. But Gideon was a coward. He took the grain down there by the winepress—way down in the valley, where no one could see him. Talk about an operation of frustration! You can just see Gideon down there pitching up the grain. When there is no wind to blow the chaff away, do you know what is happening? The straw comes falling down around his neck. I can't think of anything more uncomfortable and discouraging than to pitch up the grain and have all the straw down your back!

Well, that was Gideon, and it was at that time the angel of the Lord appeared unto him and said, ". . . thou mighty man of valour" (Jud. 6:12).

That really wasn't the proper address for Gideon, and he didn't think the angel was talking to him. I think he looked up and said, "Who me?" He was the biggest coward of all, and he was willing to admit it. "Why," he said, "I belong to the smallest tribe. My family is the small family in the tribe. And I'm the smallest potato in the family. You picked the smallest pebble on the beach—I'm a nobody."

And God said to him, "That's the reason I picked you—because you are a nobody. I want you to believe Me." We will find that God began to strengthen the faith of that man until the day came when with only three hundred men he was able to get a victory over the Midianites. Faith operated in the life of this man Gideon.

How many Christians today feel like there must be some great big show, some big demonstration, some big meeting if the ministry is going to be of the Lord? May I say to you, God doesn't move quite like that. I'm of the opinion that the greatest work for God is being done by individuals and by little groups throughout this country and around the world. I was amazed to meet a man in Lebanon who, by the way, is a member of the Gideons International. He is an active Christian layman and a real witness for Christ. You don't hear about him—he's not one who is getting publicity. And then, in the land of Israel, there is a very wonderful Hebrew Christian who has been persecuted a great deal, but he is a real witness to God. There are a great many "Gideons" around today, and they move by faith. God will use a nobody if he will trust Him. God is moving in mysterious ways His wonders to perform.

The writer to the Hebrews mentions Gideon, Barak, and Samson. I don't know whether I would have put Samson in the list or not. Samson was a real failure as far as his service was concerned, but He did believe God. There was a time when the Spirit of God came upon him and he began to deliver Israel; he never completed the job, however. The writer goes on to mention Jephthah and David (oh, we could stop and talk a long time about David!) and Samuel and the prophets. But the writer makes it clear that time would fail him to mention them all.

Now notice what all these men did—theirs was the war of faith:

> Who through faith subdued kingdoms, wrought righ-
> teousness, obtained promises, stopped the mouths of li-
> ons [Heb. 11:33].

"Stopped the mouths of lions"—we know this refers to Daniel, although he isn't mentioned by name here.

> Quenched the violence of fire, escaped the edge of the
> sword, out of weakness were made strong, waxed valiant
> in fight, turned to flight the armies of the aliens [Heb.
> 11:34].

This is the war of faith, and these are the victors.

We see now the *wideness* of faith—faith has moved into every area
of life:

> Women received their dead raised to life again: and
> others were tortured, not accepting deliverance; that
> they might obtain a better resurrection [Heb. 11:35].

"Women received their dead raised to life again"—remember the
widow of Zarephath whose son Elijah raised back to life (see 1 Kings
17:17–24).

"And others were tortured, not accepting deliverance; that they
might obtain a better resurrection." In other words, he is now talking
about martyrs.

> And others had trial of cruel mockings and scourgings,
> yea, moreover of bonds and imprisonment:

> They were stoned, they were sawn asunder, were
> tempted, were slain with the sword: they wandered
> about in sheepskins and goatskins; being destitute, af-
> flicted, tormented;

> (Of whom the world was not worthy:) they wandered in
> deserts, and in mountains, and in dens and caves of the
> earth [Heb. 11:36–38].

Here is another group of people. They didn't gain great victories out on the battlefield. They didn't enter the arena of life before large audiences and perform great feats for God. These are the "others," and they are the ones who, if you want heroes, are really God's heroes. They had trials and mockings and scourgings and bonds and imprisonment. They were stoned and they were "sawn asunder." Jerome insists that it was Isaiah who was sawn asunder, but of course that is only tradition. We don't know who suffered that cruel, horrible death. And others were tested, tempted, and slain by the sword.

I want you to notice a contrast here. Back in verses 33 and 34 when we were talking about the victories which were won, it spoke of how they "subdued kingdoms, wrought righteousness, obtained promises, stopped the mouths of lions, quenched the violence of fire, escaped the edge of the sword." They *escaped* the edge of the sword, but here in verse 37 the others were "*slain* with the sword." How do you explain this? One group by faith escaped the edge of the sword, and another group by faith were slain with the sword. We have come to a question which is still to me a very difficult subject: Why do the righteous suffer?

I know that if you are in good health today it is easy for you to toss it off and say of others, "Well, God is testing them." However, these people went through all these things *by faith*. They didn't look upon it as if they were being tested. They endured because they did it by faith. They could trust God when the day was dark, when the night was long, the suffering was intense, and when there was no deliverance for them at all.

Others were tortured; others were slain by the sword. It is wonderful to be able to get up and quote Scriptures such as Psalm 34 which says, "The angel of the LORD encampeth round about them that fear him, and delivereth them. . . . The righteous cry, and the LORD heareth, and delivereth them out of all their troubles" (Ps. 34:7, 17). That is wonderful, and God does that. But what about the "others," the others who didn't escape the edge of the sword? What about those who suffered? Stephen could look at the religious rulers of his day and say, "Which of the prophets have not your fathers persecuted?" Prophets never had it easy, my friend. Stephen himself was the first martyr to the Christian faith. Before they stoned him to death, Stephen told them, ". . . they have slain them which shewed before of the coming of the Just One; of whom ye have been now the betrayers and murderers" (Acts 7:52). And when the Lord Jesus called Saul of Tarsus, that brilliant young Pharisee, He said, "For I will shew him how great things he must suffer for my name's sake" (Acts 9:16). The Lord Jesus has also made it very clear to us, ". . . In the world ye shall have tribulation [trouble]: but be of good cheer; I have overcome the world" (John 16:33). Finally, it says of Paul and Barnabas as they went out on one of their missionary journeys that they went "confirming the souls of the disciples, and exhorting them to continue in the faith, and that we must through much tribulation [trouble] enter into the kingdom of God" (Acts 14:22).

My friend, there are a great many people who have demonstrated their faith by winning battles and by being delivered, but there are others, multitudes of them, who have suffered for the faith. Down through the long history of the church there have been the Waldensians, the Albigenses, the Huguenots, the Scottish Covenanters, and many others.

The poet Martha Snell Nickelson was a member of my church when I was pastor in downtown Los Angeles, and I had the privilege of baptizing her. She suffered a great deal—so much so that we had to baptize her in the bathtub in her own home. She screamed with pain whenever she was touched. This woman went through untold suffering before she passed on into the presence of the Lord. And right now there are literally thousands of heroes of faith lying on beds of pain. It is nice to read about walking out onto the stage of life and gaining a great victory. It is wonderful to be able to report that you have been healed. But what about those who are suffering? What about that unknown missionary out yonder on the field who is suffering for Jesus' sake? What about the minister who suffers?

Let me pass on to you something which I learned recently that deals with this question. The apostle Paul wrote, "Beloved, think it not strange concerning the fiery trial which is to try you, as though some strange thing happened unto you: But rejoice, inasmuch as ye are partakers of Christ's sufferings; that, when his glory shall be revealed, ye may be glad also with exceeding joy" (1 Pet. 4:12–13). Paul made this statement to the Colossians: "Who now rejoice in my sufferings for you, and fill up that which is behind of the afflictions of Christ in my flesh for his body's sake, which is the church" (Col. 1:24). How could Paul fill up the sufferings of Christ? Wasn't Christ's redemption for us complete and perfect? It certainly was, but there are certain sufferings that the Lord Jesus experienced in His life down here which were not redemptive sufferings. His redemptive sufferings took place on the cross—none of us can add anything to that. But you and I, if we are going to stand for Him, are going to have to pay a price for it. Some of us may have to suffer just a little.

Will you forgive me for being personal here? When I had my first bout with cancer, the Lord healed me. I rejoice in His goodness and grace and mercy to me. I have gloried in that, and I promised Him that I would give Him all the glory if He would heal me. I guess I have talked pretty loud about what God has done for me. Then I began to receive hundreds of letters from people—people who have terminal cancer and ask for prayer. I try to be faithful in remembering them in prayer. But frequently I get a letter from a loved one saying that one of these suffering saints has gone to be with the Lord. I especially remember a letter from a woman whose husband had suffered a great deal with cancer and then died. I had to take a second look at this thing. God doesn't always raise up a person from a bed of sickness. While some are healed, there are thousands today who are in the hospitals, thousands lying on beds of pain.

Do you know what the Lord did after healing me of cancer? He gave me gallstone trouble. It took a while for the doctors to even diagnose the problem, and I suffered a great deal. I think the Lord was saying to me, "I'm going to give you a thorn in the flesh so you will keep your mouth shut. You boast too much about the way I moved in your behalf. I want you to remember that I do not always heal everyone. The ones who really suffer are the greatest saints. They are the ones who know what real faith is. You don't know what it is to trust Me in a time like that." The Lord put me flat on my back, and I have never suffered as I suffered at that time. Then the Lord sent me through a battle with hepatitis, and I want to tell you, I thought He was against me. I went to

Him and talked this thing over. It was at that time that He spoke to me
from this chapter about the "others"—the others who were slain by the
sword, the others who suffered—and who did it *by faith*.

My friend, if you can walk up and give your testimony and tell how
God has healed you—and I could join you in that—or if you can get up
and say how successful you have been in business, I want to remind
you that there are multitudes of God's saints today who are *suffering*.
They are paying a tremendous price. Do you know how they are doing
it? They are doing it by *faith*. They have lots more faith than I have, and
I think they are choicer saints than I am. I have been humbled by many
a letter from some wonderful saints who are doing a work for God,
tucked away in out-of-the-way places and suffering for their faith.

The writer to the Hebrews is speaking of a company of people who
lived by faith. He simply calls them "others"—I love that! I don't want
you to forget the "others" who are today living by faith and dying by
faith. The suffering has ended for many of them, and they have already
gone into the presence of the Lord and will never have to die again.
This passage means something to me that it didn't before, and I hope it
means something new to you also.

> **And these all, having obtained a good report through
> faith, received not the promise [Heb. 11:39].**

What promise is it that they did not receive? God made many promises, and many of them received the promises that He made to them.
But *the* promise is His promise that He will raise them up and that
there will be a kingdom established here on this earth. They have not
received that promise yet, because God is still today calling out a people to His name, and, as it says here in Hebrews, "bringing many sons
home to glory." "And these all, having obtained a good report through
faith, received not the promise." We are told here the reason for that—

> **God having provided some better thing for us, that they
> without us should not be made perfect [Heb. 11:40].**

God has *us* in mind! Wasn't that gracious of Him? "That they without us should not be made perfect." God is very patiently calling people out of this world to His name—and that is the church. And until that church is completed, He is just going to keep calling them out.

We have seen in this chapter the world and the work of faith. I want to say something, and I hope I will not be misunderstood. I do not want to hear the testimony of a person who has been saved a week or a month or three months, although I *do* rejoice in their salvation. But let me illustrate my point: I got a letter the other day which told me about a man who accepted the Lord Jesus under my ministry in 1943. He had just died, and I understand that a marvelous testimony was given at his funeral as to the wonderful man of faith he was. When I am told by young people how many have accepted Christ through their witnessing, I want to say to them, "Well, it will be wonderful if three years from today or thirty years from today you can come back to me and say that these all lived and died by faith."

Some people feel that faith is something untried, something you really can't be sure of, something that doesn't really rest upon a foundation. My friend, we have had here a company of witnesses. Many of them lived long lives—they lived by faith. They found out that it works.

Again may I say that I no longer give apologetic messages, proving that the Bible is the Word of God. I just give messages from the Bible. I let the Holy Spirit minister the Word to folk. I just preach the Word of God to them and, when I do that, I receive many letters telling how their faith has been strengthened. You do not have to tell me how wonderful faith is. I am an old man now. I've been at this a long time, and you don't have to tell me this thing works. I know it works.

You see, when they made the first airplane and even when the thing flew off in the air, there were those present who said they didn't believe it and they couldn't believe their eyes. Well, there are a lot of folk today who are just as blind as a bat spiritually. They say, "I want it proven to me." My friend, if you are honest and are willing to put away the sin in your life and turn to Jesus Christ and trust Him as your Savior, then I would like to talk to you three years from today, because nobody would need to *prove* anything to you. You would *know* faith works.

There are multitudes around us right now who can say "Amen" to all of this. They already know that faith works. It's operative. It's real. It is something genuine. My friend, have you come out of the realm of make-believe and into the realm of reality? Have you found out what Jesus Christ really can do for you?

CHAPTER 12

We are in the practical section of the Epistle to the Hebrews where we see that Christ brings better benefits and duties. Chapter 11 is the *faith* chapter; chapter 12 is the *hope* chapter; and chapter 13 is the *love* chapter.

THE CHRISTIAN RACE

> **Wherefore seeing we also are compassed about with so great a cloud of witnesses, let us lay aside every weight, and the sin which doth so easily beset us, and let us run with patience the race that is set before us,**
>
> **Looking unto Jesus the author and finisher of our faith; who for the joy that was set before him endured the cross, despising the shame, and is set down at the right hand of the throne of God [Heb. 12:1–2].**

We read in the first part of this epistle of the peril of drifting; that is, of just being hearers, drifting along, and doing nothing at all about God's salvation. Now in the last part of the epistle the writer is speaking to believers of the peril of remaining stationary. He is saying, "Let's get into the race. Let's get moving and not just drift along. We are racers." I would say that one of the greatest dangers in the Christian life is the peril of just remaining stationary, of doing nothing.

When someone becomes lost in the extreme cold of the far north there is grave danger of freezing to death. The first step in that process is to fall asleep. You have to fight sleep, and you must keep moving or you will freeze to death. In a spiritual sense, the danger is the same for us as believers. We have to force ourselves to stay awake and keep moving forward in our relationship with Christ. Otherwise we will just fall asleep.

I like to tell the story about the old cowboy at one of the great camp meetings they used to have years ago in West Texas. A little lady got up and gave her testimony. She said, "The Lord filled up my cup twenty years ago. Nothing has run in, and nothing has run out." The old cowboy sitting in the back spoke out and said, "I bet it's filled with wiggletails by now!" I think that is the condition of a lot of believers today. They can say the Lord has filled their cup, but there's no running over. They've just remained that way. I agree with the cowboy, there are a whole lot of wiggletails in the cups that people are boasting of today.

"Wherefore," we are told, we are to move out, and we are to live by faith. Why? *Wherefore* is another one of these little words that cement the chapter that goes before with the chapter that is coming up—and that is what it does here. "Wherefore seeing we also are compassed about with so great a cloud of witnesses."

For many years I took the position that the "witnesses" are the Old Testament saints, many of whom are listed in chapter 11, and that they are sitting in the grandstand watching us run the race of life today. I personally couldn't think of anything more boring for them than to watch us run the Christian race down here the way some of us are running it! And I no longer believe that that is what this verse means.

When my understanding of this verse changed, it cost me the use of a marvelous illustration, but I will pass it on to you because it is a very sentimental story which does make a point. Years ago a friend invited me to the kickoff luncheon for the Rose Bowl game in Pasadena where I heard a newscaster tell this story. He told of a famous football coach in the East. The coach had a player who was known for two things. The first thing he was noted for was his faithfulness at football practice. He was the first one out and the last one to leave, but he never could make the team—he just wasn't quite good enough. The second thing he was famous for was that his father often visited him on campus and they would be seen walking arm in arm across campus, very much engrossed in conversation. Everyone noticed that and thought it was wonderful. Well, one day the coach got a telegram saying that the boy's father had died. The coach was the one chosen to tell the sad news to the boy, and so he called him in and told him. The boy was greatly shaken, of course, and had to go home for the funeral. But he was present at the next game, sitting there on the bench. Then he came over to the coach and said, "Coach, this is my fourth and last year, and I've never played in a game. I'm wondering if today you could put me in for just a few minutes and let me play." And so the coach put him in because the boy's father had just died. To his amazement, the boy turned out to be a star! The coach had never seen anyone play a better, a more brilliant game, than this boy played—so he never took him out of the game. When the game was over, the coach called the boy off to the side and said to him, "Listen, I've never seen anyone play like you played today, but up to today you were the lousiest football player I've ever seen. I want an explanation." And the boy said, "Well, coach, you see, my dad was blind, and this is the first day that he ever saw me play football."

If this Scripture means that the Old Testament saints who have gone before are sitting in the grandstand watching us run the race, then that story would be a good illustration. However, that interpretation is not accurate at all. The witnesses are not sitting in the grandstand; they are the ones who have already run the race down here. They are the ones who were down on the racetrack as you and I sat in the grandstand watching them run the race of life in chapter 11. And they ran it by faith. Those who would be called a howling success by the world ran the race by faith. And those who suffered what the world would call miserable defeat, also ran the race by faith. Although they suffered and were slain by the sword, they were just as great heroes. They all witnessed to us. We watched them as we went through chapter 11, and there were many more in the Old Testament, as the writer told us that time would fail him to tell of all of them. They witnessed to us, and encouraged us to run by faith and to live by faith.

Therefore the Christian life is here likened to a Greek race. Christ is the way to God, and along the way the Christian as a soldier is to stand firm, as a believer is to walk, but as an athlete, he is to run the race. And one day we are going to *fly*, my friend—that will be at the Rapture. We are going to do a little space travel to the New Jerusalem.

"Wherefore seeing we also are compassed about with so great a cloud of witnesses, let us lay aside every weight, and the sin which doth so easily beset us, and let us run with patience the race that is set before us." We have here another "let us" salad. Now this is not a danger signal that is put up here at all, but it is a challenge to us. Let us now get out of the grandstand; let us get down on the racecourse of life, and let us do whatever God has called us to do wherever He has called us to live and move and have our being. Let us run the Christian race, and let us move out for God. That is the whole thought here.

We are challenged to run with patience, having laid aside every weight and the sin which doth so easily beset us. God has saved us from sin. He has brought us into the heavens, actually, into the holy place, and He has made us to sit in heavenly places. He's given to us His Holy Spirit. But in spite of all that He has provided, the average Christian falls down and stumbles and wanders like a man lost in the dark. What is wrong with the Christian life as it is being lived at the present time? I will come back to the same string which I play on all the time, because I think this is the answer: the problem is that Christians do not go on with God. They get saved, give a testimony of their salvation, and that's all they ever have. They never maintain a serious study of the Word of God, which is essential to growth. They are like the little girl who fell out of bed one night. When the little girl began to cry, her mother rushed in and said, "Honey, how come you fell out of bed?" The little girl replied, "I think I stayed too close to the place where I got in." That is the problem of the Christian today. We stumble and falter and fail because we are staying too close to the place where we got in. We need to go on—this is a race, you see.

The Christian life is a race—win or lose—and it is the only race where everybody can win. Paul wrote, "Know ye not that they which run in a race run all . . ."—they *all* run to receive a prize. He went on to say, "I therefore so run, not as uncertainly . . ." (1 Cor. 9:24, 26). And again, he rebuked some of his followers saying, "Ye did run well; who did hinder you . . . ?" (Gal. 5:7).

We are encouraged by these witnesses. They are not spectators; they are testifying to us. They are in the cheering section, encouraging us to run the Christian life. Abraham is saying to you and me, "Move out by faith." Moses is saying to you and me, "Move out by faith." Daniel is saying to you and me, "Move out by faith."

Now there are two conditions to be met: "Lay aside every weight, and the sin which doth so easily beset us." What does he mean by "lay aside every weight"? Weights are highly unnecessary in a race; in fact, they are a hindrance. We ought not to be using weights.

I remember years ago when Gil Dodds, a very fine Christian, was a famous runner in this country. Some of us went out to the track at the University of Southern California, to watch him run. He ran around the track a couple of times with tennis shoes on. Then he stopped and changed into some other shoes. One of the fellows there asked why he needed to change shoes. He took one of the tennis shoes and one of the lighter pair of shoes and tossed them both to the man who had asked the question. Believe me, there was not much difference in the weight of the shoes, but just enough, he said, to cause him to lose the race.

In the Christian life there are a lot of things that are not wrong in and of themselves, but Christians should not be carrying those weights around. Why? Because you won't *win* the race. I'm going to use an illustration, but please don't think I am picking on this one particular thing, because I am not. You must determine for yourself what you can do as a child of God, and I must determine that for myself. But one young lady went to her pastor and asked, "Is it all right to dance?" Her pastor replied, "Sure it is, if you don't want to win." The point is that it is not a question of right and wrong for a Christian in his conduct—it is taken for granted that you are going to do what is right. The question is: Will it hurt my testimony? Will this keep me from winning the race? Will this be a weight in my life? There are many Christians today who are carrying around a weight they ought not to be carrying around. Don't ask me to argue with you about whether dancing is wrong. I won't argue about any of those things which separationists say you cannot do if you are Christian. I don't say you can't do it. All I'm saying is: Are you in a race? Do you want to win? Are you looking to Jesus? That becomes the important thing.

"And the sin which doth so easily beset us." What is "*the* sin"? This is not just sin in general; it is *the* sin. Again, we are cast back into the previous chapter by the *wherefore* which opened this chapter. What was the great sin in the last chapter? It was unbelief. Unbelief is *the* sin, and there is nothing which will hold you back as unbelief will. It is just like trying to run a race with the weight of a sack of wheat on your shoulder and your feet stuck inside an empty sack! You'll never be able to do it, and you cannot do it in the Christian life either. Unbelief is what holds many of us back, and if I may make a personal confession, I am confident that it has held me back more than anything else in my Christian life.

BELIEVERS ARE NOW IN CONTEST AND CONFLICT

For consider him that endured such contradiction of sinners against himself, lest ye be wearied and faint in your minds [Heb. 12:3].

The words *patience* (in v. 1) and *endured* (in v. 2) are from the same root. Trouble generally produces patience and endurance.

These Hebrew believers had come out of a religion that had a tremendous ritual and a great temple. The temple of Herod, although it was not completed even at the time it was destroyed in A.D. 70, was a thing of beauty and actually awe inspiring. Also there was a great ritual that went with it. It had been a God-given religion at the beginning, but it had been debauched and prostituted by the time this Hebrew epistle was written. Nevertheless, as far as religion was concerned, they had it. Now these believers had given up all of that; they no longer were going through all that religious ritual. They had now come to consider Him, that is, Christ, and He was everything. He was the temple. He was the ritual. He was Christianity. He was all of it. There was this simplicity in Christ, and the writer now calls them to consider Him.

They are to know what He endured when He was down here and how He learned patience. We are told in the beginning of this epistle, in the section which presented His humanity, that He learned a great many things down here although He was and is God. In the flesh He learned something which God had to experience by taking on our humanity and suffering for us. He endured and He learned patience.

"Lest ye be wearied and faint in your minds." May I say this to you very candidly: unless you stay close to the Word of God where the Holy Spirit can take the things of Christ and make them real to you, you are going to get weary of the Christian life, and you are going to faint in your minds. This is the reason there are so many discouraged Christians around today. My friend, if you come to the Word of God and get close to Jesus Christ, you are going to be encouraged. You will not grow weary of this life down here. Oh, my friend, *we* are living in the greatest days that have ever been!

Ye have not yet resisted unto blood, striving against sin [Heb. 12:4].

This simply indicates that at this time the temple was not yet destroyed. The persecution from the Gentiles of the Roman Empire which was going to come had not yet broken upon these believers. "Ye have not yet resisted unto blood."

He is saying to them, "Although you are having a very difficult time and you are having your problems and troubles, the only cure for your weakness, your weariness, your faltering, your failing, your stumbling, and your discouragement is to consider Him. Consider Christ."

> Turn your eyes upon Jesus,
> Look full in His wonderful face;
> And the things of earth will grow strangely dim.
> In the light of His glory and grace.
> > "Turn Your Eyes Upon Jesus"
> > —Helen H. Lemmel

And ye have forgotten the exhortation which speaketh unto you as unto children, My son, despise not thou the chastening of the Lord, nor faint when thou art rebuked of him [Heb. 12:5].

The writer is quoting here from Proverbs 3:11–12—"My son, despise not the chastening of the Lord; neither be weary of his correction: For whom the Lord loveth he correcteth; even as a father the son in whom he delighteth."

Their only resource was Christ—not a temple, or a ritual, or a religion. They were almost outcasts at this time, and the writer is telling them not to forget this exhortation from God to His children.

The word *children* is used in the Authorized Version, but in the Greek *son* and *sons* are used six times in verses 5–8. The Greek word for "son" is *huios,* and it means "full-grown son." Now there are a great many saints today who do not think they need to be disciplined, but discipline is for mature saints, people who have been walking with the Lord for a long time. There was a time when I had come to the place where I thought I didn't need to be disciplined anymore. I thought I had come a long ways. But the Lord put me flat on my back physically to let me know that there was some more disciplining to be done.

The word *chastening* means something a little different from what we think today. We think that chastening is punishment. The Greek word is *paideuō,* and it means "child training or discipline." You see, the Lord disciplines His own children.

For whom the Lord loveth he chasteneth, and scourgeth every son whom he receiveth.

If ye endure chastening, God dealeth with you as with sons; for what son is he whom the father chasteneth not?

But if ye be without chastisement, whereof all are partakers, then are ye bastards, and not sons [Heb. 12:6–8].

The question is sometimes asked, and it is a very pertinent question: Why do the righteous suffer? When illness confined me to my home and I spent most of my time flat on my back for about a month, I had a great deal of time to study, and I want to pass on to you what the Lord has shown me through my own experience.

Let's put this down as an axiom of Scripture: God's children *do* suffer. The Bible doesn't argue about that—the Bible just says that it is true. "Many are the afflictions of the righteous: but the LORD delivereth him out of them all" (Ps. 34:19). In the Book of Job we read, "Yet man is born unto trouble, as the sparks fly upward" (Job 5:7). The Lord

Jesus said, ". . . In the world ye shall have tribulation: but be of good cheer; I have overcome the world" (John 16:33). And even Paul said, "Yea, and all that will live godly in Christ Jesus shall suffer persecution" (2 Tim. 3:12).

Why do God's people suffer? There is no pat answer to that. No one little verse of Scripture answers it. I have gone through the Scriptures and listed seven reasons why God's children suffer. I would like to share them with you:

1. The first reason that we suffer as God's children (and even as His mature sons) is because of our own *stupidity* and our own sin. First Peter 2:20 reads, "For what glory is it, if, when ye be buffeted for your faults, ye shall take it patiently. . . ." The word *faults* refers to a sin where you missed the mark—you just didn't quite make it. "For what glory is it, if . . . ye shall take it patiently?" Peter says there is no value in the suffering which was caused by our own foolishness.

How many of you years ago invested some of your savings in a wildcat oil well in Texas? I was a pastor in Texas for many years, and I can tell you about a whole lot of folk who own dry oil wells. I know of one man in particular whose family is practically in poverty today because of such an investment. He has suffered because he played the fool.

I know another man who came to me in Los Angeles, and said, "Dr. McGee, I have certainly played the fool. My wife and I haven't been getting along too well recently. I had to work late one evening and called my wife and told her so. There is a very attractive woman in my office who has been very sympathetic toward me, and she had to work late also. All of a sudden it occurred to me that it would be nice to have dinner together. We didn't do anything but go out to dinner, and it was a friendly sort of dinner. But the wrong person was in that restaurant and saw us. He called my wife and told her. It never went any further than that, but it could have turned into a really bad thing. I played the fool." You know, a lot of saints suffer because of stupidity.

2. The second reason we suffer is for *taking a stand* for truth and righteousness. I can guarantee that if you take a stand for truth and righteousness, you are going to suffer. How many men and women could testify to that? Peter says, "But and if ye suffer for righteousness'

sake, happy are ye: and be not afraid of their terror, neither be troubled" (1 Pet. 3:14). Many people deliberately take a stand for God, and they have suffered for it.

However, we can be foolish and misguided in our thinking concerning this. One man came to me and told me that where he worked everybody was his enemy because he had stood up for God. Well, another Christian man who was an official in that same concern told me that this man was trying to lecture everybody—even during work hours! He was making an absolute nuisance of himself by attempting to witness to people while they were busy on their jobs. You see, he wasn't really suffering because he took a stand for truth and righteousness.

3. We suffer for *sin* in our lives. Paul says, "For if we would judge ourselves, we should not be judged" (1 Cor. 11:31). However, if we are God's children and refuse to deal with the sin in our lives, *God* will deal with it. He will judge us.

4. The fourth reason we suffer is for our *past sins*. "Be not deceived; God is not mocked: for whatsoever a man soweth, that shall he also reap" (Gal. 6:7). One time when I was a pastor in Nashville, Tennessee, we had Mel Trotter, the great evangelist and converted drunkard, for a series of meetings. One night after the service we all went to a place called Candyland. The rest of us got big sodas or malts, but he got a little glass of soda water. The others began to kid him about it, and he made this statement, "When the Lord gave me a new heart, He didn't give me a new stomach." Liquor had ruined his stomach, and he was still suffering because of that.

5. The fifth reason God's children suffer is for some lofty *purpose of God* which He does not always reveal to the believer. We see this in the Book of Job. Job suffered because he was demonstrating to Satan and the demon world and to the angels of heaven that he was not a timeserver, that every man does not have his price and that he loved God for Himself alone. I hope I never have to suffer as Job did.

6. The sixth reason Christians suffer is for their *faith*, as we saw in chapter 11 of this epistle. Some demonstrated their faith, and great victories were won. Some were delivered by the sword; some were slain by the sword. I think of the French Huguenots who went into

battle, knowing they would all be slain. Yet they went into battle saying, "If God be for us, who can be against us?" You see, they suffered for their faith.

7. The seventh and last reason God's children suffer is for *discipline*. That is what we have here in verse 6: "For whom the Lord loveth he chasteneth, and scourgeth every son whom he receiveth." This means child training or discipline, not punishment. Punishment is to uphold the law. A judge punishes, but a father chastens and he does it in love. God uses chastening to demonstrate His love for us. And the writer makes it very clear that you are an illegitimate child if you are not chastened by the Lord, my friend. Many people say, "Oh, why did God let this happen to me? I must not be a Christian." The fact is that your suffering is the proof that you are a child of God.

I think that if you are an intelligent Christian, when you are in trouble and do not know why, you will go to the Lord and talk to Him about it. I am sure that He will get the message to you and let you know why you are in trouble. The reason may not be that He is judging you. God does judge us, and that is punishment, but He is also our loving, heavenly Father who disciplines His children.

When I was a boy I, with several other boys at school, got into trouble. My dad came down to the school where there were several hundred children, but when he walked across that schoolyard, do you know who he was after? He was after *his* son, and he took *his son* home and disciplined him. He didn't discipline those hundreds of other children—because they weren't his. He disciplined only his boy, the boy whom he loved. My dad died when I was fourteen, and now I have a heavenly Father who does the same thing—He disciplines me in love.

Furthermore we have had fathers of our flesh which corrected us, and we gave them reverence: shall we not much rather be in subjection unto the Father of spirits, and live? [Heb. 12:9].

Believe me, I listened to my dad. I hadn't heard about the new psychology in which you don't pay any attention to your parents, and your parents aren't supposed to discipline you. My dad disciplined, and I listened to him. The writer says that if we listen to our earthly parents, "shall we not much rather be in subjection unto the Father of spirits, and live?" Whether or not you listen to your earthly father, you had better listen to your heavenly Father.

The writer to the Hebrews goes on to make a suggestion. He says, "Be in subjection to the father of spirits, *and live*." Does he mean live it up? I think he means to live a Christian life in all its fullness—that's the positive side. But I think there is also a negative aspect, which is that the heavenly Father disciplines in very severe ways sometimes, and there is a sin unto death. The sin unto death is a sin that a child of God can commit, and sometimes the heavenly Father will take a disobedient child out of this world because he is disgracing Him. The writer is saying that you had better listen to your heavenly Father because He is disciplining you in love, but if you persist in going on in sin, He may take you home.

> **For they verily for a few days chastened us after their own pleasure; but he for our profit, that we might be partakers of his holiness [Heb. 12:10].**

Sometimes I think my earthly dad got a little angry with me and vented his anger on me—but even then he did it for my profit, I'm sure. My heavenly Father disciplines me for my profit also—there is no doubt about that!

"That we might be partakers of his holiness." I believe that there is no way you can become a full-grown child of God living in fellowship with Him (that is the main thought behind "holiness") *except* through the discipline of God.

> **Now no chastening for the present seemeth to be joyous, but grievous: nevertheless afterward it yieldeth the peaceable fruit of righteousness unto them which are exercised thereby [Heb. 12:11].**

This is like the boy whose father said to him before he whipped him, "Son, this is going to hurt me more than it hurts you." The boy said,

"Yes, Dad, but not in the same place." God chastens His children. He does not get any particular joy out of it, but He does it because you and I need it. Not only does chastening not *seem* to be joyous, it *isn't* joyous, but grievous—that is our experience.

Although no chastening at the time is fun, "afterward it yieldeth the peaceable fruit of righteousness unto them which are exercised thereby." God does not discipline you without purpose.

I am reminded of the story of the man who lived in a home for the mentally ill. There was a visitor one day who saw the man beating himself on the head with a baseball bat. The visitor went up to him and said, "Why in the world are you hitting yourself on the head with the baseball bat?" The man replied, "It feels so *good* when I quit!" God does not discipline you just to make you feel good when it is over. He doesn't give you ill health just so you will appreciate good health when it returns. There is always a purpose in the discipline of God for you.

Now what is your reaction when God disciplines you? There are four reactions we can have to God's discipline that are mentioned in this chapter. I want us to take a look at each of them:

1. "And ye have forgotten the exhortation which speaketh unto you as unto children, My son, *despise* not thou the chastening of the Lord . . ." (v. 5). The first reaction is that you can despise the chastening. You can treat it lightly and accept no message from it at all. You simply become a fatalist and say, "Well, I'm having trouble. Everybody has trouble." You do not recognize the fact that your heavenly Father is disciplining you, and you do not get His message in it at all.

2. ". . . nor *faint* when thou art rebuked of him" (v. 5). There are those who respond in this way (I would call it the crybaby reaction): They begin to cry and say, "Why did this happen to me? It is not worth living a Christian life. I have served the Lord, and now He's letting this happen to me." In other words, they just faint away. Many saints take that attitude. However, when I was going through a serious illness several years ago, I received several thousand letters from people all over this country and throughout the world. Many of those people were suffering much more than I, and their attitude made me feel ashamed of myself. They had been on beds of pain for months—several of them

for *years*—and they wrote the sweetest letters I have ever read. Those letters came from folk who had real victory. We hear of meetings where people are healed and where they talk of great victories. Well, to be very frank with you, if you want to know where the great victories are being won today, go to the hospitals or visit some dear shut-in saints who have been in bed for months, and listen to them talk. You can faint, but these saints don't faint because the Lord is strengthening them.

3. "If ye *endure* chastening . . ." (v. 7). This is a dangerous response to have because it is so close to that which is true, but this is the response of the super-duper pious saints. To me they are like the Indian fakir who crawls up on a board filled with nails and lies down. He doesn't have to lie down there, but he does it. There are a lot of saints who accept the discipline of the Lord in a passive way: "Oh, this is of the Lord, and I will endure it." God never asks you to take that pessimistic, super pious attitude. If you are in trouble, why don't you go and ask Him, "Lord, why did You send this to me? There is a lesson here, and I want to learn it." Don't accept it in a passive manner, simply enduring it but complaining all the time.

4. "Now no chastening for the present seemeth to be joyous, but grievous: nevertheless afterward it yieldeth the peaceable fruit of righteousness unto them which are *exercised* thereby" (v. 11). Have you ever done sitting-up exercises? Once I became acquainted with a man who jogged around the golf course where I played golf. He was inclined to be a little chubby, so he exercised in order to lose weight. Are you exercised when you get into trouble? When you have to suffer? When an enemy comes across your pathway? Stop and ask God, "Why in the world did You let that fellow come across my pathway?" You know, God does it for a purpose. God does all these things for a purpose, and we need to be exercised by them. The apostle Paul said, "But I keep under my body, and bring it into subjection: lest that by any means, when I have preached to others, I myself should be a castaway" (1 Cor. 9:27). Paul exercised himself—that is, he didn't give in to the desires of his body—because he did not want to come before God's presence some day and be disapproved. My friend, whoever you are or wherever you are, it is time to take your sitting-up exercises.

I would like to give this word of personal testimony. A number of years ago when I had cancer, my first question to the Lord was, "Why?" It didn't take me long to discover that it was my heavenly Father punishing me—I understood that. I was a hardheaded child of God, but I got things squared away with Him. He healed me of the cancer and richly blessed the growth of our radio broadcast ministry. Then suddenly I was knocked down with another illness. The doctor told me to stay on my back, and I did so for three weeks or more. I learned something during that time which I would like to pass on to you. God wasn't judging me this time, because I've learned to keep my account short with Him. I get things straightened out with Him about every day. I do fail Him—I guess I'm still as hardheaded as I ever was—but I go to Him and confess my sin. I believe I am in the will of God. So I went to Him that second time and cried, "Lord, why in the world did You let this happen to me? I want to go on with the radio ministry." He put me flat on my back, and He said, "You are My son, and I am your Father. There are a lot of things you haven't learned yet. You may have the notion that your radio ministry is essential and that I can't get along without you, but how did I get along without you before you got here? You are going to lie here and learn something. I am your Father, and you need to learn to endure for Me. You do not know how to rest, and you do not know how to wait on Me." It took me a while, but I finally said to Him, "All right, Father, if You want me to lie here, I'll lie here. I want to learn the lesson You have for me."

We need to be exercised by the Lord's discipline, and then we will not find ourselves in the position described in the following verse—

Wherefore lift up the hands which hang down, and the feeble knees [Heb. 12:12].

Don't go through life as a Christian, complaining all the time. I used to have a friend who, when I asked how he felt, always told me how he felt—he took fifteen minutes to tell me how he felt, and he never felt good. Therefore I quit asking how he felt. He was going around all the time with his hands hanging down and with feeble knees. May I say to you, someone is watching you. How do you endure the trouble that comes from God? Do you endure it by being exercised by it? Do you say to yourself, *It is my Father, and He is chastening me. There is a purpose in it and a lesson I want to learn.* We should start our sitting-up exercises: "One, two, three. One, two, three. Lord, I'd like to know why I am suffering this way."

> **And make straight paths for your feet, lest that which is lame be turned out of the way; but let it rather be healed [Heb. 12:13].**

I'll be very honest with you and admit that I have never clearly understood what the writer meant when he said, "Make straight paths for your feet." Are we to walk the straight path so that the weak saints might follow in our footsteps? Or, are we to walk the straight path so that we don't get in the habit of limping through life? There are a lot of lamebrained Christians today who complain and criticize and are not witnesses for God at all—and yet they appear very super pious.

> **Follow peace with all men, and holiness, without which no man shall see the Lord [Heb. 12:14].**

Be encouraged and be at peace with all men; that is, with all who will let you be at peace with them. There are some people who just won't be at peace. Follow peace with all men—with all Christian men. We should make this one big cross-country race where there are a lot of us running the Christian life together.

"And holiness, without which no man shall see the Lord." If that means that I have to produce holiness, then I am going to give up, because I haven't any holiness. But, oh, the peace that I have which came through the blood of Christ! "Being justified by faith, we have peace with God through our Lord Jesus Christ" (Rom. 5:1). If I have any holiness, it is because Christ has been made unto me righteousness—*He* is my righteousness. If I get into the presence of God it will be because Christ died for me. That is encouraging, my friend. It makes me want to get out and run the Christian race.

DANGER SIGNAL: THE PERIL OF DENYING

Looking diligently lest any man fail of the grace of God; lest any root of bitterness springing up trouble you, and thereby many be defiled [Heb. 12:15].

"Looking diligently" has in it the thought of *direction*. And what is that direction? "Looking unto Jesus the author and finisher of our faith . . ." (Heb. 12:2).

"Lest any man fail of the grace of God." The word here for "fail" is not apostasy—this is not speaking of the danger of apostatizing. It means simply to fall back. In other words, a believer must keep his eyes on the Lord Jesus, not on men. If he doesn't keep his eyes on Him, he is apt to get to the place where he does not avail himself of the grace of God.

Now God has a tremendous reservoir of grace, and He wants to lavish it upon His children. He is prepared to do that, and He is able to do that. Christ paid the penalty for our sins, and God is rich in mercy, rich in grace, and He wants to expend it upon us. The problem is that many of us do not avail ourselves of His grace. But you see, we are talking here about reality—something that you can go to God for and lay hold of it. That is the glory of it all, and that is the message of this epistle. Have you gone to Him today, my Christian friend? Have you talked to Him—yes, reverently, but really talked to Him like He is your Father? Tell Him about yourself. Tell Him you need grace. We all need grace and it is available, but we've got to apply for it. We need to ask Him for it. Do not fail of the grace of God.

"Lest any root of bitterness springing up trouble you, and thereby many be defiled." One critical, ugly saint in a church can stir up more trouble than you can possibly imagine, just like one rotten apple in a barrel spoils all the others. We need to ask God for grace to endure whatever we are going through, and not become bitter toward any one or toward any circumstances.

Lest there be any fornicator, or profane person, as Esau, who for one morsel of meat sold his birthright [Heb. 12:16].

Fornication here is spiritual fornication. There is the danger of turning
from God to the things of the flesh, and it could be most anything of
the flesh. As far as Esau was concerned, it was the selling of his birthright, a spiritual birthright that entailed so much. It meant that Esau
would be in the line that led to the Messiah, and it meant that he
should be the priest of the family of Abraham. But he didn't care for it;
he was not interested in spiritual blessings.

"Profane person" does not mean that Esau cursed a great deal. It
has no reference to that at all. The word *profane* comes from two Latin
words: *pro*, meaning either "before" or "against," and *fanum*, meaning "temple." Therefore, it means against the temple or against God. It
means that Esau was just a godless fellow. He saw no need of any rec-
ognition of God, or of any relationship to Him, or of any responsibility
toward Him. So he despised his birthright and counted it as something of no value. He was even willing to trade it in for a bowl of food!
There is many a man who has sold his soul. Some have sold it for
liquor, some for drugs, some for sex, and some for dishonesty. There is
a danger for the child of God to turn from God to the things of the
flesh. We will either go forward in our relationship with Christ or fall
back—we won't stay in the same place.

> **For ye know how that afterward, when he would have
> inherited the blessing, he was rejected: for he found no
> place of repentance, though he sought it carefully with
> tears [Heb. 12:17].**

Few passages have been as misunderstood as has this passage of Scripture. It gives the impression that poor Esau wanted to repent and God
wouldn't accept his repentance. However, the writer is saying something altogether different from that. Esau despised his birthright and
then found out later that there was also an inheritance attached to it—
he would inherit twice as much as any other son of Isaac. The point is
that Esau was interested in that which was physical. When it says, "he
sought it carefully with tears," it means that he did a great deal of boo-
hooing. He was like the thief who began to weep when he was caught
and to say he was sorry. But he wasn't sorry he was a thief; he was

sorry that he'd been caught. Likewise, Esau was not repenting because he wanted to turn to God and receive His spiritual blessing. He repented because he had missed out on something material. He was actually against God.

> **For ye are not come unto the mount that might be touched, and that burned with fire, nor unto blackness, and darkness, and tempest,**

> **And the sound of a trumpet, and the voice of words; which voice they that heard entreated that the word should not be spoken to them any more:**

> **(For they could not endure that which was commanded, And if so much as a beast touch the mountain, it shall be stoned, or thrust through with a dart:**

> **And so terrible was the sight, that Moses said, I exceedingly fear and quake:) [Heb. 12:18–21].**

The writer is speaking here of the giving of the Law to Moses on top of Mount Sinai, and he is speaking of the old covenant. The people to whom he was writing were Hebrews who had turned to Christ. We need to keep that in mind all the time in this epistle. We must remember that the early church—the three thousand who were saved on the Day of Pentecost—were not Gentiles but were Jews. Until Paul and Barnabas and the other missionaries began to move out, the early church for those first few years was 100 percent Jewish.

Now these Jews in Jerusalem who had turned to Christ find themselves at a great loss. They had been accustomed to hearing the Mosaic Law read. But now they are shut away from the Law, and now they are shut out from the temple. They are no longer a part of the system at all, and they feel very much on the outside. Therefore, I think the writer is saying to them. "You come now to a mount that is different from Mount Sinai, and you do not want to go back to that." Mount Sinai was the place where the Law was given and three thousand people were slain (see Exod. 32), but three thousand people were *saved* on the Day of Pentecost. There was death at the giving of the Law; there was new life when the Gospel was preached on the Day of Pentecost. The giving of the Law was by no means a delightful experience. There were thunder and lightning, earthquake and storm, blazing fire and the blast of a trumpet that grew louder and louder and louder. It was a terrifying experience—so much so that the people said to Moses, "Speak thou with us, and we will hear: but let not God speak with us, lest we die" (Exod. 20:19). Now the writer to the Hebrews says, "You don't want to go back to that system. We have left all that behind us."

When I was a pastor in Nashville, Tennessee, there was a lady in my church who was a very lovely person, but I always felt that she was one of those Paul spoke of when he said, ". . . Silly women laden with sins, led away with divers lusts, Ever learning, and never able to come to the knowledge of the truth" (2 Tim. 3:6–7). She was a woman who was sort of a social hanger-on. She belonged to a very wealthy family, went to their cocktail parties, and engaged in their sins, but she still wanted to go to the Bible classes. She attended my church but never became a member. And she pretended to be quite a Bible student. She said to me one day after I had preached a sermon about the Law, "Dr. McGee, the giving of the Law is so beautiful, isn't it?" I had to say to that dear lady, "The giving of the Law is *not* beautiful. I think it is one of the most frightening scenes in the Bible! And it was a law that these people were told would never be able to save them. God gave them a sacrificial system whereby they could bring a sacrifice. A little animal had to die because the Law couldn't save them. The Law actually condemned them."

These Hebrew Christians had been accustomed to going to the temple and going through that ritual. Now there was nothing for them to go to, no ceremony, and no sacrifice to bring. So the writer tells them that they really do have something—

But ye are come unto mount Sion, and unto the city of the loving God, the heavenly Jerusalem, and to an innumerable company of angels [Heb. 12:22].

Remember that he is speaking to Hebrews. Mount Zion was David's place in Jerusalem. His palace was located there, and he was buried up there. Zion was David's favorite spot. Many of the Jewish believers had still been going up to the feast in Jerusalem, but the persecution had broken out, and Christians had been driven out of Jerusalem. So he assures them they have a Jerusalem in heaven. Mount Zion is the heavenly city, the eternal city of the living God. The Book of Revelation calls it the New Jerusalem. I cannot give you the number or the street name, but my future address is in the New Jerusalem. This is what we have come to by God's grace. We have something far better in Christ than the Jews ever had under the Law.

"And to an innumerable company of angels." I have made the statement—and I will stick to it—that angel ministry is not connected with the church. But we are going into the New Jerusalem some day, and the Book of Revelation shows us a huge worship scene there, a great scene which John saw and tells us about. John said in effect, "There is a company of created intelligences there, ten thousand times ten thousand of them." And then he looked around and said, "My, I didn't see that other crowd out there—there are more than any man can number." They are God's created intelligences called angels.

I have never seen an angel, but I've often wondered about them. I am going to come some day to the New Jerusalem and join with you in that great worship of the Lamb, and all these created intelligences will be there. One thing I want to do is just to talk to some of them. Wouldn't you like to talk to them? I've never had the privilege. Whenever I meet someone who tells me they have had a dream or a vision and an angel spoke to them, I tell them they ought to think back to what they had for supper the night before—that may explain the presence of an angel! You haven't seen an angel my friend; you may think you have, but you haven't. Yet the time will come when we will go to the place where they are.

> **To the general assembly and church of the firstborn, which are written in heaven, and to God the Judge of all, and to the spirits of just men made perfect [Heb. 12:23].**

"The firstborn" does not refer to Christ here, although He is called that elsewhere in Scripture. The writer is speaking of the ones who have been born again. They are the only ones who are going to be there. This is the church of firstborn ones, those who at the Rapture will be caught up to this place.

Their names "which are written in heaven, and to God the Judge of all." I thank God that when I get into the presence of "the Judge of all," there is one who will already have paid the penalty for my sins, and my record will be clear.

"And to the spirits of just men made perfect." "Perfect" does not mean complete or perfect as you and I think of it. It refers to Old Testament saints whose salvation has been made complete now that Christ has died as the Lamb of God who took away the sin of the world.

> **And to Jesus the mediator of the new covenant, and to the blood of sprinkling, that speaketh better things than that of Abel [Heb. 12:24].**

"And to Jesus"—then we are going to be brought into the presence of Jesus.

"The mediator of the new covenant." He is the mediator of the New Covenant—He is not going to thunder from Mount Sinai. Even when He was here, He sat down on a mountain and gave the law for His kingdom. I think it is going to be lots sweeter when we come into His presence some day and see Him as the mediator of the New Covenant.

"And to the blood of sprinkling, that speaketh better things than that of Abel." Abel's blood cried for vengeance, but the blood of Christ speaks of salvation. This is wonderful.

Back in verse 3 we read, "Consider him that endured such contradiction of sinners against himself. . . ." The writer is trying to get these Hebrew Christians to take their eyes off the temple, off a bloody sacrifice, off a ritual, and on to the person of Christ. Today we need to get our eyes off a church, off religion, off an organization, and off a man. No man down here should be the one to whom we are looking. Look to Jesus—look only to Him. The temple with all its splendor and ritual was passing away and was to be destroyed—now they are under a new economy.

Consider Him. Look to Jesus. Someone has said that this is the simplicity of our faith, and I agree with that, but there is a danger of over-simplification under the evangelistic methods which are being used today. I have a little book which I have entitled *Faith Plus Nothing Equals Salvation* because I believe this is true. Faith alone can save. However, today we have an epidemic of easy believism. Many folk have made salvation a simple mathematical equation: If you can say yes to this, yes to that, and yes to a half-dozen questions, then you are a Christian. This type of approach leaves no room for the work of the Holy Spirit and for the conviction of sin. It just means a nodding assent, a passing acquaintance with Jesus. It does not mean that you are born again.

There is a word that is being overworked today: *commit* your life to Christ. What kind of life do you have to commit to Christ? If you are coming to Christ as a sinner, you don't have any *life*—you are dead in trespasses and sins. The Lord Jesus is the one who said, "I have come that you might have life." *You* do not commit a life, but He committed *His life* for you and He died for you. You are dead in trespasses and sins, and He has life to offer to you: "I am come that they might have life, and that they might have it more abundantly" (John 10:10).

We also hear people say, "Give your heart to Jesus." Well, my friend, what do you think He wants with that dirty, old heart? Read the list of things He said come out of the heart (see Matt. 15:19). They are the dirtiest things that I know. He didn't ask you to give your heart to Him. He says, "I want to give you a *new* heart and a new life." We need today the conviction of sin, to know that we are sinners. We have made salvation a very jolly affair. An evangelistic crusade today is just too ducky; it's so sweet, and it's so lovely. I don't see people come weeping under conviction of sin.

> **See that ye refuse not him that speaketh. For if they escaped not who refused him that spake on earth, much more shall not we escape, if we turn away from him that speaketh from heaven [Heb. 12:25].**

"See that ye refuse not him that speaketh." Since the Lord Jesus Christ is so wonderful and since His words are very important, it pays you to give attention to Him—it will be very profitable to you.

"For if they escaped not who refused him that spake on earth,
much more shall not we escape, if we turn away from him that
speaketh from heaven." If you want to see what happened to a people
under the Law, go to the nation of Israel even today. They are not dwelling in peace. Theirs has been a really sad story for over nineteen hundred years. Why? Because they refused to hear Him. They also refused
to hear the Law, and for that God judged them. It is a serious business
not to listen to this warning. Jesus said, "If any man will do his will,
he shall know of the doctrine, whether it be of God, or whether I speak
of myself" (John 7:17). If you do His will you will find out whether it is
true or not, but if you refuse—how will you escape if you neglect so
great a salvation?

> **Whose voice then shook the earth: but now he hath
> promised, saying, Yet once more I shake not the earth
> only, but also heaven [Heb. 12:26].**

At the giving of the Law there was an earthquake, and at the crucifixion of Christ there was an earthquake. Now God is saying that the day
is coming when He is going to shake everything. When I look at the tall
buildings in downtown Los Angeles, I am tempted to say to them, "I
want to get a good look at you today because you may not be here tomorrow." God says He is going to shake the earth and heaven itself. Do
you know why He is going to do that? God is going to shake everything
to let all His created universe know that there are some things which
are unshakeable, and one of those things is living faith in Jesus Christ.
He is the Rock that we rest upon, and He cannot be shaken. Do you
want a secure place today? He is the place to go. He is the air raid
shelter that is safe today. Men want to make the world safe, but no man
can make this world safe, nor can any world organization such as the
United Nations make it safe. It is not even safe for me to walk at night
down the street on which I live. However, God is going to make it safe
some day, and in order to do that, He is first going to shake everything.

> **And this word, Yet once more, signifieth the removing
> of those things that are shaken, as of things that are**

made, that those things which cannot be shaken may remain [Heb. 12:27].

In other words, we had better be very careful that we build our lives on the right foundation. Are we building on sinking sand? Or are we building upon the Rock which is Christ?

"That those things which cannot be shaken may remain." God will remain. His word will remain, and the eternal kingdom to which believers belong will remain.

Wherefore we receiving a kingdom which cannot be moved, let us have grace, whereby we may serve God acceptably with reverence and godly fear [Heb. 12:28].

As believers we are moving toward a heavenly kingdom, but as we move toward the heavenly kingdom we need to recognize that we should be serving God down here. But how are we to serve Him? Well, we are to serve Him "acceptably." How do we serve Him acceptably? "With reverence and godly fear." My friend, Christianity is not playing church, and it is not assuming a pious attitude. It is a living, vital, and real relationship with Jesus Christ that transforms your life and anchors you in the Word of God.

For our God is a consuming fire [Heb. 12:29].

You can take that or leave it, but it just happens to be in the Word of God. This is a solemn reminder that grace is available for you to serve God, but don't trifle with God, my friend. Don't think you can play fast and loose with God and get by with it.

I remember that when I first came to Pasadena as a pastor in 1940 I was asked by a lady to go see her husband. They were a lovely couple, but the husband was sick and in bed at home. In fact, he never got out of that bed; he died there. When I went to see him, I presented the Gospel to him. He heard me courteously and then said this, "Dr. McGee, I would like to tell you right now that I accept Christ as my Savior, and I will do that, but I have trifled and played with God so often down through the years that I don't even know myself when I'm sincere and when I'm not sincere."

My friend, don't trifle with God. That day may come when you won't even know where you stand with Him at all. I tell you, our God is a consuming fire, but he is also a gracious, glorious, wonderful Savior.

CHAPTER 13

THEME: Love

As we have said, chapter 11 is the faith chapter of the Epistle to the Hebrews; chapter 12 is the hope chapter; and chapter 13 is the love chapter. Another outline that has been suggested for this section is as follows: chapter 10 the Christian's privilege; chapter 11 the Christian's power; chapter 12 the Christian's progress; and chapter 13 the Christian's practice. That is not the best outline, but it is good for chapter 13—in chapter 13 we will see the Christian's practice.

SECRET LIFE OF THE BELIEVER

Let brotherly love continue [Heb. 13:1].

"Brotherly love" should be translated as brother love. The writer of this epistle is writing primarily to Hebrews, but what he has to say has application to us. Both Jew and Gentile have been brought into one body, the body of believers. The cement, the Elmer's glue, that holds us together is brother love—not brotherly love, but brother love. We are not to love *like* brothers, but we are to love because we *are* brothers.

Now if you are a child of God you are my brother. I get many letters that say, "I am a black person. But I listen to your program and I want you to know that I am a believer and I love you." I appreciate that so much. What difference does the color of the skin make when we are children of God? When He has given us new hearts and washed us white as snow, we are brothers, we are in the family of God, and we are to love one another.

I like to illustrate the Christian life as a triangle:

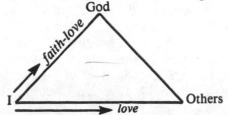

The Christian life is a life of faith and of love toward God and of love toward others. "Let *brother* love continue."

Now here is *stranger* love—

Be not forgetful to entertain strangers: for thereby some have entertained angels unawares [Heb. 13:2].

"Some have entertained angels unawares." The word *angel* may refer to superhuman beings or it may refer to human beings who are messengers from God. The same word is used to address the leaders of the seven churches of Asia Minor in chapters 2 and 3 of the Book of Revelation, in which I take the position that the "angels" are human messengers; that is, they are the teachers or leaders of the churches being addressed.

The writer mentions that there are those in the Old Testament who "entertained angels unawares." Abraham was one of them, and Jacob was another (although he didn't do much entertaining that night as he was too busy wrestling!); Joshua also entertained an angel.

The basic thought of this verse in the Hebrew epistle is that we are to extend love to strangers by showing hospitality to them. We ought to be careful that our love is exercised with judgment, but we need to recognize that there are folk around us to whom we could be very helpful. We should extend our love to them, and in doing this we might meet some very wonderful people.

Remember them that are in bonds, as bound with them; and them which suffer adversity, as being yourselves also in the body [Heb. 13:3].

Paul himself was in bonds. He knew a great deal about that, and so he says, "Remember the needy and those in trouble. Show love to those who are in need." You see, the church is a body—when one member suffers, all of us suffer. When I was seriously ill sometime ago I had the opportunity to experience this myself. A letter from one dear lady caused me to shed tears: "Dr. McGee, I'm inactive now, and I'm not able to do anything. I prayed to God that I would be able to take your disease upon myself so that you could go on with your ministry." May I say to you, we don't find that kind of spirit in every church or every group of believers, but we need it and I thank God there is a lot of it around.

We talk a great deal about the Christian fellowship which we have in our little group meetings or around the banquet table. But what about the poor saint who is off yonder lying on a bed and whom no one has visited? Many of you could have a wonderful ministry visiting the sick and lonely. This is the brother love that he is talking about here. Brother love is not something that takes place only in the church or in little groups that meet together. There has been a new phrase coined in our day: "body truth." Gracious, that truth has been in Scripture all these years; it is not something new. And you exercise that body truth by going out there to that individual who is in need. We do not hear that aspect emphasized very much today.

> **Marriage is honourable in all, and the bed undefiled: but whoremongers and adulterers God will judge [Heb. 13:4].**

"Marriage is honourable in all." The writer is condemning asceticism here. Young man, if you find a Christian girl who will have you, get married. Young lady, if you find a Christian fellow who will have you, get married. I believe that God will lead you to the right one, if you are willing to be led in that way.

Marriage is honorable in all, and sex is to be exercised within the framework of marriage. God gave marriage to mankind for the *welfare* of mankind. I know I sound like a square, because this idea of living together without being married has become very commonplace, but I must tell you, young person, that you will surely pay for it if you attempt to live together outside the bonds of marriage. The home is the very center of the whole social structure, and it is the very center of the church.

"And the bed undefiled." There is nothing wrong with sex—except that it is being taught too much in our schools today. When I was in London sometime ago, I learned that they were going to cut down on teaching sex. They found that it led to more rapes in the schools than ever before, and they felt it to be responsible for an epidemic of venereal disease.

"But whoremongers and adulterers God will judge." "Be not deceived; God is not mocked: for whatsoever a man soweth, that shall he also reap" (Gal. 6:7). This is very severe, but after years in the ministry, I have watched many Christians who have tried to get by with sexual sins, and I do not know of any who have been able to do it. Maybe they have not been detected, but they have not gotten by with it; God has judged them.

> **Let your conversation be without covetousness; and be content with such things as ye have: for he hath said, I will never leave thee, nor forsake thee [Heb. 13:5].**

"Your conversation" means your manner of life. Don't be known as a moneygrabber, as one who puts the almighty dollar above almighty God. He may not make you a millionarie, but He will never leave you or forsake you. Isn't it wonderful to have Him say that to you? It does not matter who you are or what you do, if you have responded in faith to the Word of God, you have been brought to the place where you can know that He will never leave you or forsake you. I have a notion that I have friends today who *would* forsake me, and I may have relatives who would forsake me. But the Lord Jesus will never forsake me. I hope you have Him on your side.

> **So that we may boldly say, The Lord is my helper, and I will not fear what man shall do unto me [Heb. 13:6].**

The Hebrew Christians in Jerusalem, Judea, and Samaria were going to face punishment and trials in the next few years. They needed to remember that God was not going to forsake them, and that they could say in spite of what happened, "The Lord is my helper, and I will not fear what man shall do unto me."

It is interesting to note what happened when some of the prisoners of war finally were able to return home after the war in Vietnam. Dur-

ing the war, many radicals in the United States were concerned over
the fate of the POWs, and they made trips to Vietnam and led protest
rallies on their behalf. But when the POWs were released, very few of
the radicals showed any interest in them. When the prisoners of war
came back to this country many of them testified that they had turned
to Jesus, and it was Jesus who helped them. Of course, the news media
didn't like that or want to talk about that. But Jesus never forsook
them—He stayed with them and saw them through. He is the one who
will see you through, too. I don't think the radicals or the politicians
will help you much. I am tired of listening to them. I want to listen to
Jesus, because He will never leave me nor forsake me.

SOCIAL LIFE OF THE BELIEVER

**Remember them which have the rule over you, who have
spoken unto you the word of God: whose faith follow,
considering the end of their conversation [Heb. 13:7].**

There are some ministers who use this verse and say that the members of their church are to obey them. However, it seems rather that the
thought here is of *leadership*. He is speaking of spiritual leaders, and
spiritual leaders are to lead folk to Christ. If a man is presenting Christ
and is attempting to bring people into the presence of Christ, then that
is a man to whom you should be loyal. But to be loyal to a man simply
because he is the pastor of a church is not what Paul is talking about at
all.

**Jesus Christ the same yesterday, and today, and for ever
[Heb. 13:8].**

"Jesus Christ." There is no accident in the Word of God; that is, no
word is ever used carelessly. *Jesus* is His human name; *Christ* is His
title, that which speaks of His deity.

Jesus is the name which links Him with mankind. It identifies Him
as the most wonderful person in this world.

Jesus, Name of sweetness,
  Jesus, sound of love;
Cheering exiles onward
  To their rest above.

Jesus, oh the magic
  Of the soft love sound;
How it thrills and trembles
  To creation's bound.
                    —Author unknown

How wonderful Jesus was as a person when He was down here.
People crowded around Him because He was so human. The mobs
followed Him and they loved Him. It was the *teaching* of Jesus they
hated—it was not Jesus the man. *He* was wonderful, my friend.

Christ is a title which speaks of His messianic mission to this
earth—He is God manifest in the flesh, "Jesus Christ"—how marvel-
ously these two are meshed together here. He is Jesus Christ, and He is
the same.

I feel inadequate to deal with this very marvelous verse, but I do
want to say that it has probably been misapplied as much as any verse
in the Word of God. There are many who use this verse and say, "When
Jesus was here nineteen hundred years ago, He performed miracles;
therefore we ought to perform them today. He healed nineteen hundred
years ago, and so we ought to be healing today. He is still in that same
business."

Jesus Christ *is* the same, but we need to understand *how* He is the
same. He is the same in His character, in His person, and in His attributes, but He is not the same in place or in performance. When I was in
the land of Israel I didn't see Him over there. I saw very little evidence
at all of Him in that land. Over nineteen hundred years ago He was in
Bethlehem as a little baby, but He is no longer a baby and He is not in
Bethlehem. Later He was a little boy playing in the streets of Nazareth,
but I didn't see Him. I saw a lot of little boys, but He was not one of
them. A few years later as a man He walked through that land, and He
did heal. I was in Jerusalem and I saw Golgotha, but there is not a cross
there and He is not on a cross today. The whole thought of this epistle

is that He is now at the right hand of God: ". . . We have such an high priest, who is set on the right hand of the throne of the Majesty in the heavens" (Heb. 8:1); and we are to look "unto Jesus the author and finisher of our faith . . ." (Heb. 12:2). He accomplished our redemption nineteen hundred years ago, and He sat down at the right hand of God. Right now He is up yonder, but some day He will come as the King to the earth to establish His kingdom. He has not yet called His church out of the world, but some day He will do that. You see, Jesus is not the same in place and performance, but He is the same in His attributes.

When He was here nineteen hundred years ago, He was God who came down to our level. When I have been in the land of Israel and have considered that fact, I have truly marveled at it. He came to a place where there was no great wealth or pomp or ceremony. He did not come to Rome, the center of power and government. He did not come to Athens, the great cultural center. He did come to an insignificant outpost of the Roman Empire, and He came to the level of the common man.

Because we are often afraid that we will be misunderstood when we speak of Christ's humanity, we do not emphasize it as we should. Rather, we emphasize His deity, and we need to do that because the liberal speaks of nothing but His humanity, and even that he does not truly understand. But in His humanity, I think that Jesus was the most attractive person who ever walked this earth—not because He was God, but because He was a man, a real man.

Have you ever wondered why the crowds were attracted to Him and followed Him? He was strong but gentle—so gentle that little children came to Him. However, He could drive the money-changers out of the temple and they ran for cover, because He was *man* enough to put them out. Also He was attractive. He had what we call today charisma. People followed Him because they loved Him, and they knew they were in the presence of a man who *was* a man. In Capernaum He healed a leper and then had to leave because the crowds pressed around Him, so that He couldn't even continue His ministry. Even publicans and sinners came to Him, which was the thing that so angered the religious crowd. If He came to your town today—I hate to say this—I don't think He would come to your church. I have a notion you would find Him where the crowd is; He would be mixing with people and probably holding a child or two. When He went to Jericho at the end of His ministry, again we find that the crowds lined the way so that little Zacchaeus had to climb up a tree in order to see Him, but even there our Lord stopped and brought him down out of the tree. How sensitive the Lord Jesus was to human need, and how wonderful He was in His person!

I want to say something very carefully: it was the *person* of Christ that appealed; it was not His *teachings*. His great declaration that He was going to die to redeem men was not popular. At the very beginning of His ministry, it was His teaching that offended. He taught that He was the Bread of Life and that He had come to give His life that men might have spiritual food, and added, "Therefore said I unto you, that no man can come unto me, except it were given unto him of my Father." And John's record tells us, "From that time many of his disciples went back, and walked no more with him. Then said Jesus unto the twelve, Will ye also go away? Then Simon Peter answered him, Lord, to whom shall we go? thou hast the words of eternal life" (John 6:65–68). The crowd narrowed down, and only twelve stayed with Him. Why? Because of His teaching. And actually Simon Peter rebuked Him when He spoke of His impending death, ". . . Be it far from thee, Lord: this shall not be unto thee" (Matt. 16:22). Even His loyal disciples didn't like that kind of teaching. When men came into contact with the Lord Jesus Christ, they found grace and truth; they found sweetness and strength; they found meekness and majesty; they found light and love. He appealed to men, but when He died on a cross that cross became an offense. The cross is still an offense, but Jesus is still attractive.

It is said that when Savonarola in the city of Florence went before the great populace and said, "Be free," they applauded him. But when he said to them, "Be pure," they ran him out of town. They refused his teaching when it did not appeal to them. The Lord Jesus said to men, "You have to turn from sin. You cannot live in sin. I have come to make you free, but I will have to give My life for you and you will have to come as sinners to Me." And sinners came—when men were desperate, they would come to Him. I believe that is the only way men will come to Him even today.

I wish that I could present Him as He really was nineteen hundred years ago when He came to this earth. How wonderful He was! Today, your sorrow is His sorrow, and your joy is His joy. He will be the same in the future—"the same yesterday, and to-day, and for ever." He is never going to change. Some day we will be in His presence. How wonderful that will be!

Before we leave this subject, let me share with you an excerpt from a booklet written by Dr. C. I. Scofield, entitled *The Loveliness of Christ*:

> First of all, as it seems to me, this loveliness of Christ consists in His perfect humanity. Am I understood? I do not now mean that He was a perfect human, but that He was perfectly human.
>
> In everything but our sins, and our evil natures, He is one with us. He grew in stature and in grace. He labored, and wept, and prayed, and loved. He was tempted in all points as we are—sin apart. With Thomas, we confess Him Lord and God; we adore and revere Him, but beloved, there is no other who establishes with us such intimacy, who comes so close to these human hearts of ours; no one in the universe of whom we are so little afraid. He enters as simply and naturally into our twentieth century lives as if He had been reared in the same street.

He is wonderful, my friend, and you ought to know Him. Paul, who came to know Him, found that even at the end of his life he wanted to know Him better. He said, "That I may know him, and the power of his resurrection . . ." (Phil. 3:10). Today my one ambition is to know Him and to get out His Word—I cannot think of anything better to do.

> **Be not carried about with divers and strange doctrines. For it is a good thing that the heart be established with grace; not with meats, which have not profited them that have been occupied therein [Heb. 13:9].**

It is amazing that most of the cults today go in for special diets. I believe that food is important as far as the health of the body is con-

cerned, but it has nothing to do with your relationship to God. Paul
wrote, "But meat commendeth us not to God: for neither, if we eat, are
we the better; neither, if we eat not, are we the worse" (1 Cor. 8:8). He
is saying the same thing here. Do not go off into these strange cults and
teachings in which diet and ceremonies and rituals and little study
groups are supposed to make you a super-duper saint. Nothing in the
world is going to build you up but the Word of God. The Word of God
will build you up if it brings you to the person of Christ, and only the
Holy Spirit can take the things of Christ and make them real unto you.

> **We have an altar, whereof they have no right to eat
> which serve the tabernacle [Heb. 13:10].**

A comparison is being made here between what Israel had under the
old covenant in contrast to the better things of the New Covenant. Believers today have an altar, but this altar is not the Lord's Supper as
some people have mistakenly interpreted it to mean. We do not have a
material altar with a local address, but we have an altar which is in
heaven. It is the throne of grace up yonder. It was a throne of
judgment—He condemned us there—but now that the blood has been
placed there, we can come and find grace and salvation.

I would like to say at this point that Christian fellowship is not a
church banquet. For years while I was in the ministry I heard it said:
"Come to the banquet. We are going to have some marvelous Christian
fellowship." No, you're not, my friend. You are just going there for a
good time and to fill your little tummy. The only place you can have
real Christian fellowship (koinōnia) is around the Word of God. It is
the Word of God which brings you to the person of Christ and enables
you to see Him in all His glory. It is then that you will have fellowship
and a good time with other believers. Our Lord is wonderful, my
friend—it is terrible to pass Him by.

> **For the bodies of those beasts, whose blood is brought
> into the sanctuary by the high priest for sin, are burned
> without the camp [Heb. 13:11].**

The writer is referring to the sin offering. When Christ died it was for the fact that you and I are sinners. Not only do we commit sin, we are sinners by nature, and He took our sins on Himself that He might give us a new nature.

> **Wherefore Jesus also, that he might sanctify the people with his own blood, suffered without the gate [Heb. 13:12].**

Jesus died outside the city. Why? Because He was the sin offering. The sin offering was taken away from the temple and "burned without the camp." Jesus was our sin offering, and He paid the penalty for our sin.

> **Let us go forth therefore unto him without the camp, bearing his reproach [Heb. 13:13].**

The writer is saying to these Hebrew Christians, "Don't mind leaving the temple. Don't mind leaving the rituals. Those things are not helpful. Go to Him—Go to Christ."

My friend, we, too, are to go to Him. We are on our way to a heavenly Jerusalem. This is real separation he is talking about here. Today we put the emphasis on separation *from*; we are separated from something—that is, "I don't do this and I don't do that." Real separation is not *from*; it is *unto*. Paul said he was separated *unto* the Gospel, separated *unto* Christ, separated *unto* the Word of God. In fact the word *Hebrew* means the "one who crossed over." Abraham was called a Hebrew because he had come from the other side of the Euphrates River, signifying that his old life was gone. The children of Israel crossed the Red Sea, and they were delivered from slavery; they were redeemed, and a new life was then possible. Then they had to cross the Jordan River to live in the Promised Land, the land of Canaan, the kind of life that we also should live down here.

We are to go "without the camp, bearing his reproach." The Hebrew Christians hated to leave the temple and their religion. Many people today are wrapped up in "churchianity," thinking that because they are members of a church they are saved. They need to get away from ritual and religion and come to Christ. Come to Him—that is real separation, and that is real salvation.

> **For here have we no continuing city, but we seek one to come [Heb. 13:14].**

Again the writer makes it clear that we have nothing permanent down here.

SPIRITUAL LIFE OF THE BELIEVER

> **By him threfore let us offer the sacrifice of praise to God continually, that is, the fruit of our lips giving thanks to his name [Heb. 13:15].**

A child of God is a priest today and can bring sacrifices to God. There are four sacrifices of a believer. (1) You can sacrifice your *person* (see Rom. 12:1). Someone has said, "When one truly gives himself to the Lord, all other giving becomes easy." (2) You can sacrifice your *purse* (see 2 Cor. 8:1–5). If He doesn't have your purse, He doesn't have you. (3) You can offer the sacrifice of *praise*, which we find in this verse: "By him therefore let us offer the sacrifice of praise to God continually, that is, the fruit of our lips giving thanks to his name." (4) Finally, you can offer the sacrifice of *performance* or doing good, which we find in the following verse—

> **But to do good and to communicate forget not: for with such sacrifices God is well pleased [Heb. 13:16].**

When you took that basket of fruit over to that dear, lonely, and sick child of God whom everyone has forgotten about, you were a priest offering a sacrifice to God. It was well pleasing to Him—He took delight in your doing that. Again I must refer to the time when I was seriously ill and flat on my back. At that time I received many letters from folk who were lots worse off physically than I was. They wrote lovely letters, and every one of them was a sacrifice. And many folk helped me in a tangible way, and that too was a sacrifice well pleasing to God. My friend, if Christianity does not walk in shoe leather it is no good at all. The Lord Jesus is up yonder at the right hand of God—that is where He is as Head of the church—but His feet are down here right where the rubber meets the road. He wants Christianity to be in shoe leather, and He would like to walk in your shoes.

Obey them that have the rule over you, and submit yourselves: for they watch for your souls, as they that must give account, that they may do it with joy, and not with grief: for that is unprofitable for you [Heb. 13:17].

We had this same thought in verse 7. If your pastor is a man of God who is teaching the Word of God then you are to obey the Word of God as he has given it to you. It would be better to not hear the Word of God, than to hear it and not obey it.

Pray for us: for we trust we have a good conscience, in all things willing to live honestly [Heb. 13:18].

"Pray for us." Evidently the readers of this epistle knew the writer, and I believe the writer was Paul.

"For we trust we have good conscience, in all things willing to live honestly." It is wonderful to pillow your head at night with a good conscience, a conscience enlightened by the Word of God. A great many people are not walking in the light. "If we say that we have fellowship with him, and walk in darkness, we lie, and do not the truth: But if we walk in the light, as he is in the light, we have fellowship one with another, and the blood of Jesus Christ his Son cleanseth us from all sin" (1 John 1:6–7).

But I beseech you the rather to do this, that I may be restored to you the sooner [Heb. 13:19].

This statement also makes me believe that Paul wrote this epistle. Apparently he was in prison at this time, and he is saying to these Hebrew

Christians, "I want to come back and be among you again"—after all, he was a Hebrew himself.

BENEDICTION

Now we come to the benediction, a benediction which I have used thousands of times in my ministry.

> Now the God of peace, that brought again from the dead our Lord Jesus, that great shepherd of the sheep, through the blood of the everlasting covenant,
>
> Make you perfect in every good work to do his will, working in you that which is well-pleasing in his sight, through Jesus Christ; to whom be glory for ever and ever. Amen [Heb. 13:20–21].

"That great shepherd of the sheep." The Lord Jesus is here called the Great Shepherd. In Psalm 22 He is presented as the Good Shepherd, and in John 10:11 He calls Himself the Good Shepherd. As the Good Shepherd He gave His life for the sheep. As the Great Shpeherd He is the one who perfects the sheep and builds them up. We see that here and also in Psalm 23. He leads us beside the still waters and leads us to the place where the grass is good and green and very tender, that is, to the Word of God. Then in Psalm 24 He is presented as the Chief Shepherd. "And when the chief Shepherd shall appear, ye shall receive a crown of glory that fadeth not away" (1 Pet. 5:4). He died in the past as the Good Shepherd; He is the Great Shepherd today; and He is coming some day as the Chief Shepherd for His sheep. He started out with one hundred sheep, and do you know how many sheep He is going to have with Him in heaven? Ninety-nine? No. He is going to have all one hundred sheep with him there.

"Through the blood of the everlasting covenant." Christ's blood is the basis of every covenant God has ever made.

"Make you perfect"—this has been the purpose of the Epistle to the Hebrews. We have been told, "Let us go on to perfection." He means for us to go on to maturation, to being full-grown children of God. It is marvelous to admire a little baby lying in the crib, but if you come back in twenty years and he is still lying there, saying, "Da-da-da," something is radically wrong. There are a lot of such saints who need to come to maturation, to grow up, and the Epistle to the Hebrews will help them to do that.

"In every good work to do his will." What is the important thing for a child of God? To do His will—to allow Him to work His will in your life, "working in you that which is well-pleasing in his sight, through Jesus Christ; to whom be glory for ever and ever. Amen."

> **And I beseech you, brethren, suffer the word of exhortation: for I have written a letter unto you in few words [Heb. 13:22].**

Notice how personal this is. I have to smile when he says he wrote this "in few words." To my judgment this is a long letter, but he calls it "few words."

> **Know ye that our brother Timothy is set at liberty; with whom, if he come shortly, I will see you [Heb. 13:23].**

Again, this sounds like Paul. Apparently Timothy had been in prison. A note in my Bible at the bottom of this chapter says, "Written to the Hebrews from Italy by Timothy." That is not part of the text, but is some man's interpretation. This man could be wrong, and I could be wrong in saying that Paul wrote this epistle. The important thing is that the Holy Spirit wrote it and that He takes the things of Christ and shows them unto us.

> **Salute all them that have the rule over you, and all the saints. They of Italy salute you [Heb. 13:24].**

The writer was in Italy, and so was Paul.

He closes this epistle with a wonderful benediction, and I will close with it also. I cannot improve on it because it interprets itself—

Grace be with you all. Amen [Heb. 13:25].

APPENDIX

THEME: The authorship of Hebrews or did Paul write Hebrews?; internal evidences on authorship; date and destination; arguments available on authorship; a defense of the Pauline authorship

THE AUTHORSHIP OF HEBREWS OR DID PAUL WRITE HEBREWS?

The Epistle to the Hebrews presents many moot problems. Some of them are in conjunction with the question of authorship, which we shall consider under the following divisions:
1. Internal evidence on authorship
   (Is Hebrews an epistle or treatise?)
2. Date and Destination
3. Arguments available on authorship
4. A defense of the Pauline authorship

It is evident that we are contending for the Pauline authorship of Hebrews. First we shall present all arguments against it, as indicated by the headings. Then we shall present the evidence that establishes the Pauline authorship in our own thinking.

INTERNAL EVIDENCES ON AUTHORSHIP

The deciding factor in determining the authorship, according to one writer, is that tradition and history shed no light upon the question of the authorship of Hebrews. This probably is being considered first because we do not agree with the writer on this statement. Rather, we believe that both history and tradition lend a deciding voice to this question.

We are therefore thrown back, in our search for the author, on such evidence as the epistle itself affords, and that is wholly inferential. It seems probable that the author was a Hellenist, a

Greek-speaking Jew. He was familiar with the Scriptures of the
OT and with the religious ideas and worship of the Jews. He
claims the inheritance of their sacred history, traditions and in-
stitutions (1:1), and dwells on them with an intimate knowledge and enthusiasm that would be improbable, though not
impossible, in a proselyte, and still more in a Christian convert
from heathenism. But he knew the OT only in the LXX [Septua-
gint] translation, which he follows even where it deviates from
the Hebrew. He writes Greek with a purity of style and vocabu-
lary to which the writings of Luke alone in the NT can be com-
pared. His mind is imbued with that combination of Hebrew
and Greek thought which is best known in the writings of
Philo. His general typological mode of thinking, his use of the
allegorical method, as well as the adoption of many terms that
are most familiar in Alexandrian thought, all reveal the Hellen-
istic mind. Yet his fundamental conceptions are in full accord
with the teaching of Paul and of the Johannine writings.

The central position assigned to Christ, the high estimate of
His person, the saving significance of His death, the general
trend of the ethical teaching, the writer's opposition to asceticism and his esteem for the rulers and teachers of the church,
all bear out the inference that he belonged to a Christian circle
dominated by Pauline ideas. The author and his readers alike
were not personal disciples of Jesus, but had received the gospel from those who had heard the Lord (2:3) and who were no
longer living (13:7). . . . The letter [Paul] quotes the OT from the
Hebrew and LXX but Hebrews only from LXX. . . . For Paul the
OT is law, and stands in antithesis to the NT, but in Hebrews the
OT is covenant, and is the "shadow" of the New Covenant. (*The
International Standard Bible Encyclopedia,* vol. II, p. 1357.)

We have quoted voluminously from this writer because his main thesis
is to show that Paul could not have been the author. His sole proof is
based on the internal evidence from the epistle.

In considering the internal nature of the epistle, a word must be
said relative to the question: Is it really an epistle? There is no word of

salutation or greeting in this Epistle to the Hebrews, such as marks the other New Testament books, with the possible exception of 1 John. It is in the form of a treatise rather than a letter. In it are long, philosophical sentences written in purest idiomatic Greek. It bears no mark of a translation from the Hebrew, as Clement of Alexandria suggests. This is an inference on his part because it was written to Hebrew-speaking Jews. The length of the epistle is another thing that might suggest a treatise, yet note the author's own words in this respect, ". . . for I have written a letter unto you in few words" (Heb. 13:22). Delitzsch has this onlightening comment to make on this epistle:

> We seem at first to have a treatise before us, but the special hortatory reference interwoven with the most discursive and dogmatic portions of the work soon show us that it is really a kind of sermon addressed to some particular and well known auditory; while at the close the homiletic form changes into that of an epistle.

According to Deissmann's definition of an epistle as distinct from a letter, we feel sure that this would allow it to fall under the category of an epistle. Its conclusion is that of an epistle. Later in our discussion we shall present a reason for the omission of a greeting. These problems are intimately tied up with the question of authorship, especially when one attempts to maintain the Pauline authorship. We agree with Plumer that this is an epistle.

As we conclude this section on the internal nature of the Epistle to the Hebrews, we should note that this epistle is in composition and lofty concept the masterpiece of the New Testament, although there is no conclusive evidence for the authorship. Only suggestions and intimations shed light on this problem. In our defense for the Pauline authorship we shall undertake to show that the suggestions and intimations point to Paul as the author, yet we are not dogmatic in stating that the proof is positive.

DATE AND DESTINATION

The latest date for the composition of Hebrews is A.D. 96. The earliest date cannot be determined so easily. It must have been written after

A.D. 50 if it is made dependent on Paul's epistles. All critics fix the dating between these two terminal points. Moffatt shows that Clement, Justin Martyr, Hermas, and Tertullian knew of it and quoted from it. Clement quoted from it at length. By the second century it was widely circulated and read. Rees places the date around A.D. 80, Moffatt around A.D. 85. Here is a list of the probable datings: Basnage—A.D. 61; L'Enfant and Beausobre—A.D. 62; Horne and Bagster—A.D. 62 or 63; Pearson, Lardner, Tomlin, Mill, Wetstein, and Tillemont—A.D. 63; Authorized Version and Lloyd—A.D. 64; Michaelis—A.D. 64–65; Scott—A.D. 65; Ebrard before A.D. 58. The number of dates given suggests that the means used to arrive at a date was by way of the lottery, not by process of scholarship. However, Hebrews must have been written before the destruction of Jerusalem in A.D. 70. Because there is constant reference to the Old Testament ritual being in progress at that time, certainly there would have been reference to the destruction of the temple. Having examined the arguments carefully, we are fully persuaded that those who place the dating of it after the destruction of Jerusalem do not sufficiently answer the question of why the writer omitted reference to this catastrophe.

E. Schuyler English gives us this word:

> It is also obvious that the epistle was written before the destruction of Jerusalem in A.D. 70. For at the time of its composition Mosaic institutions were still being observed—priests were offering gifts according to the Law (8:3–5) and the temple was still standing (13:11–12). The temple was in Jerusalem.

Godet has a fitting comment:

> This epistle, without introduction or subscription, is like the great High Priest of whom it treats, who was without beginning of days or end of years, abiding an High Priest continually. It is entirely fitting that it should remain anonymous.

The epistle was first accepted by the Eastern church. Athanasius accepted it, and the council of Carthage confirmed it in A.D. 397. Paul's name was on the epistle about the time it began to circulate.

The consensus is that Hebrews was written to Jewish Christians. But where were the Jewish Christians located? It was not written for the whole body of Jewish believers everywhere. It was written to a particular church located in a particular place. The epistle bears testimony to this: The church had for some time obeyed the Gospel (Heb. 5:12); past conduct inspired confidence in their sincerity (Heb. 6:9); they had been kind to God's people (Heb. 6:10); note other personal references in Hebrews 10:32–34; 13:19, 23. Was this church in Palestine or out of Palestine? It is around this question that the argument on destination is based.

First of all, there is evidence that the first readers were Jews. The epistle assumes an intimate knowledge with the Old Testament. The readers were of the same lineage as Jews in the Old Testament (Heb. 1:1; 3:9). Zahn has this comment to make:

> Hebrews does not contain a single sentence in which it is so much as intimated that the readers became members of God's people who descended from Abraham, and heirs of the promise given to them and their forefathers, and how they became such. 13:13 shows that both the readers and author were members of the Jewish race.

Now we shall try to determine whom or rather what particular church the author was addressing. This epistle is addressed to the *Hebrews*, which word in the New Testament does not apply to all Jews. It was used for those who were more thoroughly of Jewish origins and habits and who spoke the vernacular of Palestine. The other Jews outside of Palestine were designated Hellenists. Lindsay says that Acts 6:1 makes this distinction clear. DeWette says that Eusebius, speaking of the Jews of Asia Minor, styles them not Hebrews but *ex Hebraion ontes*. Chrysostom says that this epistle was sent to Jerusalem. The fact that the epistle was written in Greek does not negate the evidence that it was sent to Palestine, for it is natural for a writer out of Palestine to write in the universal language of his day. The Palestinian Jews were well acquainted with Greek, as Deissmann has clearly demonstrated. In fact, it was the language of communication. DeWette held to the opinion that this epistle was destined to parts other than Palestine; yet he acknowledges that the Jewish character of the epistle—the persecutions which they were enduring, the consequent risk of apostasy, and the ancient opinion—reveal Palestine as the more probable destination. Ebrard wrote, "We are at liberty to seek these Jewish Christians only in Jerusalem."

ARGUMENTS AVAILABLE ON AUTHORSHIP

We can say with Shakespeare that we have now come to the very heart of the matter. There is less evidence for the authorship of this epistle than of any other book of the New Testament. Others have problems of authorship, but there is some definite evidence available and some general agreement, at least, regarding the author. For example, nearly all critics say that some John wrote the fourth Gospel. But there is no such agreement regarding Hebrews. Moffatt rightly says that few characters in the New Testament have escaped the attention of those in late days who have sought to identify them as the author of Hebrews. Apollos, Peter, Philip, Silvanus, Prisca, Barnabas, and Paul have all been suggested as the possible author. To Moffatt's list we might add the names of Luke, Silas, Clement of Rome, Ariston, and Titus, all of whom have been suggested as the possible author. Out of this dozen, one is privileged to take his choice—or refrain from doing so, as Moffatt does. Moffatt concludes that the author was one of those unknown personalities in whom the early church was more rich than we realize. There is absolutely no basis, other than conjecture, for asserting that most of these were the author, although several have a plausible claim.

As we examine their claim to authorship, Luke and Clement are easily eliminated because a comparison of their writings to the Epistle to the Hebrews reveals a difference in style, composition, and influence. Clement quotes from Hebrews, and his own writings show marked differences. (See introduction of Moffatt's commentary on Hebrews.) So little is known of the others, with the exception of Barnabas, that it is impossible to establish a case for or against them. Barnabas will be considered in the three theories that are presented.

In the early church were three traditions regarding the authorship of Hebrews: The Alexandrian tradition supported the Pauline authorship; the African tradition supported the authorship of Barnabas; Rome and the West supported the idea that it was anonymous.

1. *Alexandrian tradition:* Clement says that his teacher, probably Pantaenus, explained why Paul did not address his readers under his name. He further states that Paul wrote it in Hebrew and Luke translated it into Greek. Origen follows Clement, but knowing that the view of Alexandria was criticized, he concludes that the author is "known only to God." By the fourth century the tradition of the Pauline authorship was well established in Alexandria, Syria, and Greece. This tradition prevailed until the revival of learning. Eusebius favored the Pauline tradition, as did Dionysius of Alexandria, Alexander of Alexandria, Athanasius, Cyril of Jerusalem, Epiphanius, the Council of Laodicea of A.D. 363, and Erasmus. Among those who denied the Pauline tradition were Irenaeus, Cyprian of Carthage, Tertullian, Caius and Novatus, presbyters of the church at Rome. Calvin did not accept the tradition, for he says, "I, indeed, can deduce no reason to show that Paul was its author." Luther and Moll defend the authorship of Apollos against the Pauline tradition. Thus we see that tradition was probably equally divided.

2. *African tradition:* This view supported Barnabas as the author of Hebrews. Tertullian was the leading exponent, for he attributed the epistle, without question, to Barnabas. This is the most tempting suggestion, as Wickham remarks. It suits the character of Barnabas. Barnabas was a "Levite of the country of Cyprus," a Hellenist by birthplace, but a Hebrew by race, interested in the sacrificial system, companion of Paul (yet one who entertained views of his own), the "son of consolation," the mediator and peacemaker between old and new. Zahn infers that this tradition arose in Montanist churches and originates in Asia. However, this tradition was superseded by the Alexandrian tradition, for in A.D. 393 the council of Hippo reckoned thirteen epistles to Paul, but in A.D. 419 the council of Carthage reckoned fourteen to Paul, which would include Hebrews.

3. *Roman tradition:* This view said the author was anonymous. No tradition of authorship appears before A.D. 400, according to Rees. Stephen Gobarus, writing in A.D. 600, says that both Irenaeus and Hip-

polytus denied the Pauline authorship. The epistle was known to
Clement of Rome, and he mentions no one as author. Another suggestion as to the authorship of Hebrews is mentioned by Plumer. It is that
of Zemas, the lawyer. This makes thirteen guesses as to the author of
Hebrews.

A DEFENSE OF THE PAULINE AUTHORSHIP

We are not holding dogmatically or tenaciously to an obsolete view.
Rather, we have examined the evidence and find no reason to reject the
Pauline authorship. It is not our purpose in this section to affirm that
Paul wrote Hebrews, but to set forth our reasons for tentatively accepting the Pauline authorship, or the authority, that this epistle rests
upon, for the canonicity of this epistle depends largely upon the view
of authorship. It was accepted into the canon on Pauline authority; and
with that removed, it is possible to reject this great epistle.

Under the first heading (Internal Evidences on Authorship) we attempted to show that all the light from the epistle itself reveals only the
fact that the author is anonymous. His name is nowhere mentioned in
the epistle. Now, using the internal evidence, we want to show how
Paul *could be* the author.

So far we have tried to show two things: (1) there is no evidence,
external or internal, to support any claim as to the authorship, except it
be Paul; (2) there is nothing incompatible with thinking that Paul
wrote it.

Now we shall take our third burden of proof and attempt to show
that internal and external evidence support the Pauline authorship.

1. *Internal Evidence:* Origen remarked that the thoughts
(*noemata*) of this epistle all bore the stamp of Paul's mind, but the
language was *Hellenikotera*, purer Greek than his. Following is Lindsay's list of representations and images which are found in Hebrews
and in Paul's other epistles, which are not found in the works of other
New Testament writers.

Compare Heb. 1:1, 3 with 2 Cor. 4:4; Col. 1:15–16.

Compare Heb. 1:4; 2:9 with Phil. 2:8–9.

Compare Heb. 2:14 with 1 Cor. 15:54, 57.

Compare Heb. 7:16, 18–19 with Rom. 2:29; Gal. 3:3, 24.
Compare Heb. 7:26 with Eph. 4:10.
Compare Heb. 8:5; 10:1 with Col. 2:17.
Compare Heb. 10:12–13 with 1 Cor. 15:25.

DeWette and Bleek have concluded that since Hebrews reads more like Paul's writing than any other New Testament writings, it was written by a disciple of Paul. The opponents of the Pauline authorship are quoted to show that this book is not unlike Paul's writings and could have been written by Paul. Paul obviously meets this requirement.

Some have claimed that Hebrews 2:3 excludes Paul as the author because he says in Galatians 1:11–12 that he received his Gospel not from men but from God. However, this is not incongruous with Paul's statement in Galatians. Paul is evidently using the editorial "we" that is used so effectually in the New Testament. If Paul places himself in the same category with the other Christians at Jerusalem, he could not say that *we* received it from God on the road to Damascus about midday on a mule. Paul's conversion was peculiar to himself. Then the Galatians passage does not exclude the fact that Paul did not have it confirmed unto him by the ones who heard the Lord. In Galatians he is defending his apostleship and is therefore showing from whence he received his authority.

As to the statement that Hebrews 13:7 reveals that the apostles were no longer living at the time Hebrews was written, we can hardly see where this verse establishes any such view.

Regarding the fact that the Epistle to the Hebrews quotes the Old Testament from the Septuagint Version, it is possible for Paul to have quoted only from the Septuagint in Hebrews and from both the Septuagint and the Hebrew in his other epistles. The fact that there are more quotations in this book than in any other New Testament book shows that the author is placing a great deal of stress on these quotations. Instead of quoting from memory, he would have a copy of the Old Testament at hand. Paul did quote from the Septuagint frequently, and he could easily have used it exclusively in the Epistle to the Hebrews.

Rees says that Paul's Christology turns about the death, resurrection, and living presence of Christ in the church. In contrast, the Epistle to the Hebrews centers about the high priestly nature of Christ's work. He evidently is thinking of Ephesians, Colossians, 1 Corinthians, and Romans, for the rest of Paul's epistles deal no more with these subjects than does Hebrews. This method of trying to distinguish different authors by difference of style is not conclusive, to say the least. Certainly it is not a valid argument in this epistle.

We come now to the problem of the absence of the author's name in the Epistle to the Hebrews. Why did the author conceal his name? The theory has been advanced that had Paul been the author he would have subscribed his name, and the fact that his name does not appear shows he did not write it. We submit Plumer's answer to this sort of reasoning:

> Moreover, if Paul is proven not to be its author because it lacks his name, the same reasoning would prove it had no author at all, for it bears no name whatsoever.

Now let us examine the reasons why Paul might have concealed his name. Dr. Biesenthal, writing on Hebrews, advances a new and interesting theory for the reason the writer concealed his name. He shows that Christianity's teaching that animal sacrifices were no longer needed was being felt in heathendom. Consequently, sacrifices at births, marriages, and other occasions, were being neglected. The priestly class, which lived by these sacrifices, and the large cattle industry, were being threatened by utter ruin. This created a great antagonism against Christianity. Dr. Biesenthal, a Hebrew by race, concludes that for this reason the writer withheld his name from this epistle which so bitterly denounces animal sacrifices.

Also Paul himself was a man who was hated by the Jewish nation. To them he was no less than a traitor. This brilliant young Pharisee, who was well versed in the ritual of Moses, as he himself claims, was anathema to his brethren in the flesh. In writing to them this learned work, composed in the best Greek, he withheld the name that would prevent its circulation among those to whom it was originally destined.

There is another reason we think to be more valid, which was presented even by the Alexandrian tradition. It is that Paul left off his salutation, "Paul, an apostle of Jesus Christ," because he was not the apostle to the Jews but to the Gentiles. Another more recent suggestion on this line comes from a consideration of Hebrews 3:1: ". . . Consider the Apostle and High Priest of our profession, Christ Jesus." Christ is the great Apostle in this epistle and the writer would not subscribe his name beside the one of Christ. Certainly the fact that the writer did not mention his name does not eliminate Paul from the list of possible authors.

There are a few suggestions in the epistle that point to Paul as author. The writer was a Jew acquainted with the details of Mosaic ritualism (Heb. 13:13). He was acquainted with Greek philosophy, or rather, Alexandrian thought. The author of this epistle had been in prison in the locality where the ones addressed resided (Heb. 10:34). He was at that time in prison in Italy (Heb. 13:19, 24). Timothy was his companion and messenger (Heb. 13:23). When Paul was in Rome in prison he used Timothy to carry messages, and he sent him on a trip from the west to the east (Phil. 2:19). The writer hoped to be liberated (Heb. 13:19). This is the same thought that is expressed in Philippians 1:25 and Philemon 22. While these suggestions are not conclusive, who better fits this description than Paul? An appropriate supposition from Lightfoot concludes this section on internal evidence: "The very style of it may argue the scholar of Gamaliel."

The dating of the Epistle to the Hebrews does not conflict with the Pauline authorship. If it were written before the destruction of Jerusalem, which we believe to be correct, it coincides nicely with Paul's imprisonment at Rome. Paul's last visit to Jerusalem helps explain the epistle. The Book of Acts tells us that Paul went up to Jerusalem in spite of the warning of the Spirit. His arrest was the result of having gone into the temple to purify himself with the four men who had a vow. This he was asked to do and to make apparent that he walked orderly and kept the Law. Did he do wrong? This is not a question for us to answer. The point is that he—knowing that he was dead to the Law—acted through zeal and love for his brethren. The believers at Jerusalem still clung to the Law and to the temple. When Paul was in Rome, he wrote this epistle to show these Jews the better things of the New Covenant and to warn them not to be drawn back into Judaism.

This throws a great deal of light on Hebrews 13:13: "Let us go forth therefore unto him without the camp [Judaism], bearing his reproach."

The Spirit of God could have used this epistle for the comfort of Jewish Christians right before the destruction of the temple. We suggest this to show that the dating and destination are not incompatible with the Pauline authorship.

2. *External Evidence:* Several of the early church fathers who favored the Pauline authorship have been mentioned, but we have reserved for this section other evidence that confirms us in our view that Paul wrote Hebrews. This is Origen's statement in full regarding the author of Hebrews.

> The thoughts are Paul's but the phraseology and composition are by someone else. *Not without reason have the ancient men handed down the Epistle as Paul's,* but who wrote the Epistle is known only to God.

We especially note that clause which is italicized. Evidently there was already in Origen's day a tradition that Paul wrote this epistle. Quite evidently it was the opinion of the earliest church in the East that Hebrews was Paul's epistle. It was not until a later day, and by a church more remote from Palestine, that the tradition arose of another author. Jerome, the greatest of the Latin fathers, considered Paul the author. It was during the third and fourth centuries that the Pauline authorship was denied in Rome. It is also interesting to note that during this same period the epistle was held in disrepute. After it regained its place as canonical Scripture, it was also considered as Pauline. Lindsay makes this valuable comment on the Western tradition. Jerome suggests that at first it was received in Rome as Scripture and received also as Pauline. It is significant that both go together.

Others could be mentioned, but they would add nothing decisive either way.

We now turn to a bit of evidence that is enlightening. Peter wrote to those of the circumcision, to believing Jews everywhere. In 2 Peter 3:15 he mentions the fact that Paul had written to them. He separated this epistle from the others of Paul (v. 16). No epistle of Paul other than

Hebrews answers to this statement. If Hebrews is not the epistle, then the epistle to which he refers has been lost.

To conclude our remarks, we quote a statement from Weymouth that illustrates how easy it is to defend a theory and support it with misinformation:

> The only fact clear as to the author is that he was not the Apostle Paul. The early Fathers did not attribute the book to Paul, nor was it until the seventh century that the tendency to do this, derived from Jerome, swelled into an ecclesiastical practice. From the book itself we see that the author must have been a Jew and a Hellenist, familiar with Philo as well as with the Old Testament, a friend of Timothy and well known to many of those whom he addressed, and not an Apostle but decidedly acquainted with Apostolic thoughts; and that he not only wrote before the destruction of Jerusalem but apparently himself was never in Palestine. The name of Barnabas, and also that of Priscilla, has been suggested, but in reality all these distinctive marks appear to be found only in Apollos. So that with Luther, and not a few modern scholars, we must either attribute it to him or give up the quest.

This statement is very sweeping, incorrect, and superficial. He does not even present the facts.

While we do not dogmatically assert our thesis of the Pauline authorship with any such note of certainty, we do not see fit to change our view without sufficient evidence. We still believe it to be reasonable to accept the Pauline tradition.

We deplore the fact that the King James Version carries the heading, *The Epistle of Paul the Apostle to the Hebrews.* It should read, *The Epistle to the Hebrews.* Such is the tenet that we affirm in this paper.

BIBLIOGRAPHY FOR APPENDIX

Calvin, John. *Commentary of Paul the Apostle on Hebrews.* 1567 Reprint. Grand Rapids, Michigan: Baker Book House, n.d.

Edwards, T. C. "The Epistle to the Hebrews," *Expositor's Bible.* Grand Rapids, Michigan: Baker Book House, n.d.

Gaebelein, Arno C. "The Epistle to the Hebrews," *The Annotated Bible.* Neptune, New Jersey: Loizeaux Brothers, n.d.

International Standard Bible Encyclopedia, article on the Epistle to the Hebrews. Grand Rapids, Michigan: Wm. B. Eerdmans Publishing Co., 1925.

Lindsay, W. *Lectures on The Epistle to the Hebrews. International Critical Commentary.* Edinburgh, Scotland: T. & T. Clark, 1867.

Moffatt, James. "The Epistle to the Hebrews," *International Critical Commentary.* Edinburgh, Scotland: T. & T. Clark, 1924.

Plumer, William. *Commentary on Paul's Epistle to the Hebrews.* Carlisle, Pennsylvania: The Banner of Truth, n.d.

Wickham, E. C. *Epistle to the Hebrews.* London, 1910.

BIBLIOGRAPHY

(Recommended for Further Study)

Bruce, F. F. *The Epistle to the Hebrews*. Grand Rapids, Michigan: Wm. B. Eerdmans Publishing Co., 1964.

DeHann, M. R. *Hebrews*. Grand Rapids, Michigan: Zondervan Publishing House, 1959. (Message given on the Radio Bible Class)

English, E. Schuyler. *Studies in the Epistle to the Hebrews*. Neptune, New Jersey: Loizeaux Brothers, 1955.

Hoyt, Herman A. *The Epistle to the Hebrews*. Winona Lake, Indiana: Brethren Missionary Herald Co., n.d.

Hughes, Philip Edgecumbe. *A Commentary on the Epistle to the Hebrews*. Grand Rapids, Michigan: Wm. B. Eerdmans Publishing Co., 1977.

Ironside, H. A. *The Epistle to the Hebrews*. Neptune, New Jersey: Loizeaux Brothers.

Kelly, William. *An Exposition of the Epistle to the Hebrews*. Addison, Illinois: Bible Truth Publishers, 1905.

Kent, Homer A., Jr. *The Epistle to the Hebrews*. Grand Rapids, Michigan: Baker Book House, 1972. (Excellent)

MacDonald, William. *The Epistle to the Hebrews*. Neptune, New Jersey: Loizeaux Brothers, 1971.

Meyer, F. B. *The Way into the Holiest*. Port Washington, Pennsylvania: Christian Literature Crusade, 1893. (A rich devotional study)

Murray, Andrew. *The Holiest of All*. Old Tappan, New Jersey: Fleming H. Revell Co., 1894. (Excellent devotional treatment)

Newell, William R. *Hebrews, Verse by Verse*. Chicago, Illinois: Moody Press, 1947. (Excellent)

Pfeiffer, Charles F. *The Epistle to the Hebrews*. Chicago, Illinois: Moody Press, 1962. (Good, brief survey)

Phillips, John. *Exploring Hebrews*. Chicago, Illinois: Moody Press, 1977.

Thomas, W. H. Griffith. *Hebrews: A Devotional Commentary*. Grand Rapids, Michigan: Wm. B. Eerdmans Publishing Co., 1962. (Excellent)

Vine, W. E. *The Epistle to the Hebrews*. London: Oliphant, 1957.

Wiersbe, Warren W. *Be Confident*. Chicago, Illinois: Moody Press, 1977.

Wuest, Kenneth S. *Hebrews in the Greek New Testament for English Readers*. Grand Rapids, Michigan: Wm. B. Eerdmans Publishing Co., 1947.